A FORWARD STEP

Educational Backgrounds for Police

A FORWARD STEP

Educational Backgrounds for Police

By

DONALD E. CLARK, A.B.

Sheriff, Multnomah County
Portland, Oregon

and

SAMUEL G. CHAPMAN, A.B., M.A.

Assistant Director
The President's Commission on
Law Enforcement and Administration of Justice
Washington, D. C.

CHARLES C THOMAS • PUBLISHER
Springfield · Illinois · U.S.A.

Published and Distributed Throughout the World by
CHARLES C THOMAS • PUBLISHER
Bannerstone House
301-327 East Lawrence Avenue, Springfield, Illinois, U.S.A.
Natchez Plantation House
735 North Atlantic Boulevard, Fort Lauderdale, Florida, U.S.A.

© *1966, by* CHARLES C THOMAS • PUBLISHER
Library of Congress Catalog Card Number: 66-16789

With THOMAS BOOKS *careful attention is given to all details of
manufacturing and design. It is the Publisher's desire to present books
that are satisfactory as to their physical qualities and artistic possibilities
and appropriate for their particular use.* THOMAS BOOKS *will be true
to those laws of quality that assure a good name and good will.*

Printed in the United States of America
RV-1

INTRODUCTION

This text is dedicated to the man whose distinguished career has taken him to the Deanship of American police administrators. His record is concisely briefed by the *San Francisco Chronicle:*[1]

EXPLODED FOLK LORE

IT IS AN AMERICAN CONCEPT that the ivy-covered professor is to be viewed with distrust, an impractical fellow protected by his academic robes and his book shelves from reality.

Orlando W. Wilson was an academic fellow. He was dean of the University of California's school of criminology at Berkeley four years ago when he was summoned to Chicago where the police department was, in the words of a press service report, "traveling a bumpy road to corruption."

WILSON, A GRADUATE of the university in 1924, was a rookie cop under the late, great Berkeley Chief August Vollmer when Vollmer was creating his force of "college cops." His interests, however, have been primarily with the university and his reputation was made while serving on its faculty.

When he took the challenging job of straightening out the 11,000-man Chicago department, there were sneers, and the opposition of the entrenched. He arrived when public confidence was at low ebb and after eleven officers had been charged with stealing property they had sworn to protect.

He has just been commended by the International Association of Police Chiefs for "outstanding success" in his reorganization and rejuvenation. Wilson has weeded out the bad guys by the score, removed his department from the influence of ward-heelers, and instituted the use of one-man patrol cars and police dogs.

There are scores of exceptions to that old myth about the academic ineffective. We add the name of Orlando Wilson to their roster.

---

[1]*The San Francisco Chronicle* 44:1, August 24, 1964.

PREFACE

This book is about standards and why a college education should be adopted as a minimum requirement for policemen. In order to better appreciate the issues and arguments that lie ahead, the reader should recognize at the outset the distinction between education and training. These two concepts tend to blur because of semantic confusion and because they are closely related, often used interchangeably.

As a standard but useful point of departure, let us look briefly at a few selected dictionary definitions. Education is defined as "the process of training and developing the knowledge, skill, mind or character . . . especially by formal training." Training means to "instruct so as to make proficient or qualified . . . to discipline or condition." It is obvious from these excerpts that training is the narrower term. For our purposes, those of making a valid case for college-educated policemen, an education is considered as theoretically, not vocationally, oriented. The focus is broad, and the individual is exposed to a wide range of thought that better allows social phenomena and developments to be seen in their proper perspective and tempers judgment with understanding.

Training, in the sense it is used herein, denotes learning or instruction that is more specific, more "how to" or procedurally oriented. An education provides a broad framework of social reference while training provides the means to more effectively reach a given goal or perform a given task. Both are indispensable to the police, but training cannot fill an educational void. Education is essential if our society is to produce police with an understanding of their role in a fast changing world and in whose judgment each citizen may trust. At the same time, this individual must be effectively trained as a police officer. Education serves to build the whole man; training arms him to execute his function in the most efficient manner. Neither process, of course, can or should cease when a recruit graduates from the basic training academy.

It should be readily recognized by the citizen and the professional police officer alike that the training aspect changes rapidly and radically. Much of what passed for police training years ago has changed or become obsolete. Social and technological change is constant, which forces training to adapt to the situation. This pattern will continue. In years hence, then, an individual educated in the broader disciplines with the wider perspective will possess the advantage. His education, his frame of reference, is still valid. Not only will he be better equipped mentally and attitudinally to change with the times, he will more likely be one whose efforts have helped to change the times. He is less prone to forming final conclusions and knows the folly of closing one's mind.

Where do standards fit into the picture? They determine what the police service will be and what it will achieve tomorrow and, more significantly, in the years to come. Not long ago we saw standards that emphasized physical size, courage and local residence to the near exclusion of education or intellectual capacity. One can cite many reasons why this was so, but time and necessity have modified the approach and will continue to do so. Today the selection process occupies a much higher position in the police scheme of things. Professionalization, new tools, both scientific and social, and the growing complexities of the job will serve to generally heighten standards and increase the importance of personnel selection.

Gene S. Muehleisen, Executive Director of the California Commission on Peace Officer Standards and Training, summarized the police dilemma in an address at Kent State University, Kent, Ohio, on November 21, 1964:

> We are proud to have been the thin blue line of defense, but we have been on the "defensive" too long. We are now afforded the opportunity to take the offense through highly-selected, well-educated, and adequately-trained police. We need them on the beat, in the laboratory, in the front office and in our research and educational systems. Today's police officer is confronted with the strange contradiction of a more educated, more sophisticated, yet more lawless public. Unfortunately, his task has become extremely complicated. He is no longer a purist as an enforcer of the law. Today he is confronted with an astonishing range of human problems, legal dilemmas and social changes which demand unusual skills and knowledge.

This book posits that higher education and the police service are compatible. It also posits that minimum educational standards for preservice entry into the police field will continue to be elevated. The book presents the reasoning which prompted the Multnomah County Sheriff's Police Department to ask for the elevation of its minimum preservice entry educational standard. It also presents material which was used to document and support the request for elevated standards. Furthermore, it summarizes press reaction to the proposals, legislative support which speaks to elevated educational standards, summarizes police education in England and Wales, and concludes by asserting that it is important that the police recruit men and women who are academically better prepared for a career in the public service than has been the case in the past.

DONALD E. CLARK
SAMUEL G. CHAPMAN

CONTENTS

A FORWARD STEP

Educational Backgrounds for Police

Chapter 1

ESCALATION OF STANDARDS IN MULTNOMAH COUNTY

When one considers the anatomy of the police department, he imagines such component parts as modern equipment, adequate headquarters facilities and a large pool of personnel. Of the three items, by far the most important and the most expensive is the latter—manpower. It has been shown that a limited number of personnel, adequately equipped and housed and carefully selected, can provide a superior level of police service.

It was to improve the police service in Multnomah County and assure its future which prompted Multnomah County Sheriff's police executives to submit a letter to the Multnomah County Civil Service Commission on June 7, 1965, requesting that a minimum educational standard of a baccalaureate degree be established for service as a deputy with the sheriff's police department. After considering the request and hearing testimony during its regular meeting on June 8, 1965, the three-member Civil Service Commission set the matter over for a month. At its meeting of July 13 the Commission acted favorably upon the request, causing the Multnomah County Sheriff's Police Department to become the first large nonfederal law enforcement agency in the United States to require baccalaureate degrees of applicant deputies. The requirement was to become effective with the next scheduled deputy sheriff civil service examination, anticipated during the fall, 1965.

The civil service meeting of June 8, 1965, was the meeting which actually saw the request over the hill. During the meeting five men testified before the Civil Service Commission. All spoke in support of the sheriff's request for raising the minimum educational requirement to a baccalaureate degree. These were Dr. Frank Roberts, assistant to the President of Portland State College and long time Multnomah County

3

resident; Undersheriff Samuel G. Chapman; Portland Police Bureau Captain J. Bardell Purcell, representing the Oregon State Advisory Board on Police Standards and Training; and Sheriff Donald E. Clark.

The fifth speaker proved the evening's highlight. Dr. A. C. Germann offered a carefully prepared, impeccably presented series of remarks of justification. Dr. Germann, Professor of Police Science at California State College, Long Beach, is America's foremost authority on police personnel administration and a scholar who has diverse experience in the academic world. Dr. Germann's background also includes combat service in the United States Army Air Force in Europe during World War II and postwar duty with the Los Angeles city police as a patrolman.

Following Dr. Germann's presentation, the Civil Service Commission asked numerous questions of the sheriff and Dr. Germann, all of which were fielded concisely and with alacrity. The Civil Service Commission, all three members present, seemed ready to render a decision on the request at the June 8 meeting, but ultimately set the matter over five weeks for further deliberation.

Only two Civil Service Commission members were present to enact business at the July 13 meeting. These were Chairman Donald C. Walker, attorney at law and secretary of the Portland Beavers Professional Baseball Club, and Mr. S. Eugene Allen, dean of the Evening School at Portland's Multnomah College. The third member, Mr. Harry E. White, Vice-President of the First National Bank of Oregon, was ill and unable to attend.

Following routine business, the matter of elevating standards was quickly and favorably agreed upon after a minimum of discussion from the floor. The highlight of the floor discussion was a strongly worded oral statement by Multnomah County Police Union President, Detective Allen E. McDaniels, who urged that the proposal be favorably received. Following favorable action, President McDaniels congratulated the sheriff, his staff and the commission.

After passing the sheriff's request, Commissioner Allen

and Chairman Walker addressed some general comments to the concept of college-educated police officers and the evening's board action.

Chairman Walker inquired whether there would be sufficient applicants if the requirement was elevated. He also asked in rhetorical fashion if the office of deputy sheriff would offer sufficient challenge for a baccalaureate degree holder. He was concerned that there would be frequent resignations following a short term of service. Thirdly, Chairman Walker acknowledged that since crime was on the increase and since there was a constant increase of population, perhaps the law enforcement agencies with the higher-qualified personnel might be able to widen the scope of law enforcement by seeking means of deterring crime rather than focusing greater attention upon the detection and apprehension of law violators. He highlighted the question of emphasis of mission. Finally, Chairman Walker said, "I hope very much that the new requirements bring forth the results that are anticipated. I am very hopeful that this will occur and we certainly would appreciate knowing the progress you make as the months go by."

Commission member Allen noted that:

Modern law enforcement clearly requires the highest order of character, professional training, and education. The rights of citizens are, to a very considerable extent, in the hands of law enforcement personnel. This personnel must therefore be prepared to understand the traditions, the legal basis, the cultural and moral heritage, and the ages-old struggle that led to the establishment of these human rights under our laws. Moreover, the concept of the law enforcement officer must change from the traditional attitude toward the "cop on the beat" to the more appropriate and modern concept of a well-trained expert in the field of the social sciences—psychology, sociology, political science, economics, history, and all of the understandings that are required for effective prevention of crime as well as its detection.

Certainly a four year college education—particularly in the social sciences and the liberal arts—increases the understanding of the law enforcement officer. It enables him to do a better job than would be the case without such educational background. I am delighted to support the recommendation of the Sheriff and to place Multnomah County in the forefront of this effort toward better enforcement and improved administration of law.

Nonetheless there are some practical considerations that cannot be escaped nor ignored. My enthusiasm for raising standards and for placing college-trained persons in these responsible positions is qualified to some extent by these considerations.

Unless the public is willing to pay for the high quality of public service sought and required under this new standard we may find two serious problems facing us:

(1) Inadequate pay (and Multnomah County's present schedules are inadequate for college trained and qualified deputy sheriffs) may well result in the "culls" and those who have managed to secure the degree (which is by no means difficult today) but who are incapable of doing acceptable work at the higher and appropriate salary schedules applying for and receiving appointments to the sheriff's force.

(2) The first danger is accompanied by the other which is that the new degree requirement will effectively prevent|able, mature, intelligent, and conscientious persons who, because of circumstances have been unable to complete four years of college, from taking the examinations and thus being considered.

In short, my reservations stem from the fact that I lack confidence that we are willing to pay the kind of salaries that are earned and demanded by properly qualified people. Such salaries would be substantially higher than I think we are likely to offer. If this is so I am concerned on the two scores set out above.

I think it important, however, that we make a start and that citizens support the necessary salary increases demanded by such improved standards of public service. I hope for the best and commend the sheriff for the sincere work he is doing to bring the highest possible level of public service from his department to the citizens of the county. I am glad to vote for the proposal.

In an interview a week following the July meeting, commission member White asserted that he viewed the principle of higher standards for police compatible with law enforcement needs in these days of social change. However, he was concerned that the recruiting base may be unduly restricted by the adoption of the degree requirement. Mr. White wondered if there was not room for a condition which would enable candidates who had completed around three years of university study to compete, and if successful be appointed with an understanding that within a specified period they complete the requirements for the baccalaureate degree or be terminated. Mr. White, whose assignment with First National Bank of Oregon is Vice-President in charge of personnel, was pleased that the department had the opportunity to seek degree holders, but would view the results of testing and the performance of men recruited with much interest.

The landmark decision of July 13, 1965, was preceded by a significant elevation in standards which the Civil Service Commission formalized at its meeting of July 1, 1964. At that meeting

the Civil Service Commission elevated the minimum educational
standard from a requirement which said:

Ninety quarter hours or 60 semester hours from an accredited college or university; or a high school graduate with two years service with a recognized
Government Police Agency.

To an educational requirement which called for:

Ninety quarter hours or 60 semester hours from a college or university as
accredited by one of the six regional or several professional accrediting
bodies listed in "Lovejoy's College |Guide".

When the incumbent sheriff assumed office on January 5,
1963, the minimum educational standard for service as a deputy
with the Multnomah County Sheriff's Office was a high school
diploma or its equivalent.

The following chapters of this book are presented so that
the circumstances leading to the establishment of the four-year
degree requirement are fully documented and not obscured by
the sands of time. They also present relevant material which
speaks to educational standards and the police service. This
book is prepared so that an event which should have enduring
effect on police standards in the United States is recorded in
fact and does not fall to the realm of folklore.

Remaining chapters include an overview of the Multnomah
County Sheriff's Office; an accurate account of the request of
June 7, 1965, asking for the elevated standard; local press
coverage including editorials; legislative support for higher
standards in the police service; the educational standard picture for constables in England and Wales; and letters from knowl-
edgeable commentators in both public and nongovernmental
circles urging the adoption of the baccalaureate requirement.

Chapter 2

MULTNOMAH COUNTY SHERIFF'S OFFICE ORGANIZATION

Multnomah County, Oregon, was organized as a political sub-division in 1854, five years prior to Oregon's admission to the Union. The first records of the sheriff's office in Multnomah County date to 1859. In 1916 the Columbia River scenic highway was completed, a considerable portion of which lies in Multnomah County. About this time the sheriff's office uniform patrol was formed. This organization continued to grow approximately consistent with the county's population. Today the 244-man sheriff's police department provides the full range of law enforcement service at a per capita cost greatly below that of most American municipalities of comparable size.

In 1960 the population of Multnomah County was 521,112 persons of whom 144,284 resided in the rural areas. The county is 424 square miles in area, with 74 square miles in Portland. Of the remaining 350 square miles, about 100 square miles are heavily populated or industrial in nature, the remaining portion being rural, agricultural or forested lands. The elevation ranges from sea level to over 4,000 feet in the east part of the county.

Oregon law requires that the sheriff's office be established at the location designated by the county commissioners for the holding of courts. Oregon law designated the sheriff as the chief executive officer in his respective county, and the office is provided for by the state constitution. The duties of the sheriff are enumerated as follows:

1. Arrest and commit to prison all persons who break the peace or attempt to do so and all persons guilty of public offense.

2. Defend his county against those who by riot or otherwise endanger the public peace or safety.

3. Execute the process and order of the courts of justice or of judicial officers when delivered to him for that purpose, according to law.

4. Execute all warrants delivered to him by other public officers according to law.

5. Attend the terms of the supreme, circuit or county court held within his county and to obey its lawful orders or directions.

The sheriff is also the tax collector for the county and, at the command of the presiding judge of the circuit court, opens circuit court at each monthly session. The organization of the Multnomah County Sheriff's Office is shown below.

The sheriff's executive office is headed by the sheriff, who is aided by an administrative assistant, one personal secretary, an office accountant and one business manager. By legislation at the state level, the sheriff's office is organized into three separate departments: (1) police; (2) tax collection; and (3) civil process. The number of personnel authorized for each department in the 1965-66 fiscal year include the following:

1. Tax Department   54
2. Civil Department   13
3. Police Department   244
   plus Executive Office.   5

TOTAL   316

The fifty-four tax department employees are supervised by a chief deputy who is directly responsible to the sheriff. This department collects all of the taxes from sixteen governmental bodies and groups functioning in Multnomah County. This includes tax collections for the City of Portland and all school districts. Total taxes collected in 1965-66 were in excess of ninety million dollars.

The sheriff's civil department is supervised by a chief deputy who also is a member of the Oregon state bar. This department handles process emanating from both circuit and district courts, such as service of divorce papers, attachments, evictions, garnishments, liens, foreclosures on real and personal property, seizures and many other matters pertaining to civil law.

Neither tax nor civil department personnel are affected by the Civil Service Commission decision concerning baccalaureate

CHART I

ORGANIZATION OF THE MULTNOMAH COUNTY SHERIFF'S OFFICE

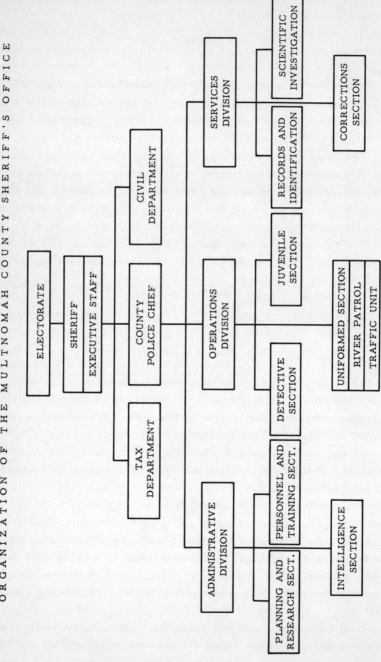

degrees; only police department personnel are subject to the standard.

THE SHERIFF'S POLICE DEPARTMENT

The police department consists of three divisions: (1) administrative; (2) operations; and (3) services. Each division is supervised by a veteran police captain who, as division commander, is designated as deputy chief.

Administrative Division

The administrative division includes three sections: (1) inspection and planning; (2) personnel and training; and (3) intelligence.

The inspection and planning section is staffed by a lieutenant who assists and implements decisions effecting the present and future administrative policies of the department. He conducts survey and research projects for the department.

The personnel and training section is headed by a lieutenant who is in charge of all personnel records and related confidential files. His duties include supervising and planning the in-service and recruit training programs designed for members of the department. Police work is today approaching professional status. While it may be some years before this objective is achieved, the educational preparation and on-the-job training of police officers will contribute materially to the recognition of law enforcement as a profession.

Since the Multnomah County Sheriff's Office is moving progressively toward professionalization, the duties of the personnel and training officer become highly important in discharging this responsibility. Department emphasis on training has further resulted in motivating large numbers of officers to pursue college and university academic courses and to enroll in law school. This schooling is accomplished by individuals during their off-duty hours.

The department has actively sought and sponsored nationally known schools in Multnomah County and has presented departmental schools in areas of need and special competence. These activities have attracted students from police agencies both within and outside the state of Oregon. The personnel and training section coordinates, guides and supervises every aspect of their presentation.

The intelligence section is supervised by a lieutenant and consists of five deputies who make various criminal investigations. Assignments include vice control, narcotics investigations and routine work such as personnel (background) investigations, processing liquor license applications and so forth. This is a specialized field and personnel must be adaptable to be effective. This section maintains close liaison with all other law enforcement agencies, local, state and federal, concerning joint vice and intelligence operations.

Operations Division

The deputy chief in charge of the operations division supervises 136 persons who perform the line and investigative functions of the police department. The division includes the following three sections: (1) uniform; (2) detective; and (3) juvenile.

The uniform section is commanded by a captain in charge of three lieutenants, seven sergeants and eighty-three deputies.

This section includes two small but important specialized units: (1) traffic enforcement and (2) river patrol.

The traffic enforcement unit is primarily concerned with selective traffic enforcement. It is staffed by ten uniformed deputies supervised by a sergeant. Patrol is maintained by the use of both automobiles and solo motorcycles. In December, 1964, personnel of this unit began using the radar equipment which augments the standard enforcement equipment used by traffic officers.

In Oregon the sheriff of each county is charged with enforcing the boating laws on all waters within his county. In Multnomah County there are eighty-one miles of the Columbia and Willamette Rivers to patrol. This includes eleven miles of the Willamette River in the City of Portland upon which, in the course of patrol, the boat crews enforce the state boating laws. County jurisdiction on the Columbia River extends as far east as Bonneville Dam.

The detective section of the operations division conducts

the continuing investigations of all crimes and incidents reported to the sheriff's police. Detectives follow up leads provided by the uniform and other sections. This section is also responsible for the service of criminal warrants, those either sent in from outside jurisdictions or issued in Multnomah County. Prisoners upon arrest are booked in the county jail, later conducted to court for arraignment or for trial, guarded during the trial and returned to the jail at recess of court or at the conclusion of the case. Twenty-four hours after receipt of the judgment order prisoners are transported to the Oregon state penitentiary or correctional institution at Salem.

The detective section is also required by order of the presiding judge of the circuit court to transport the grand jury on its monthly inspection of the Portland Police Department and county institutions. Juries are also conducted to crime scenes before indictments are returned or during trials. Criminal subpoenas are served by the detective section upon witnesses required to testify before the grand jury. The detectives also return prisoners from other states, such expense being audited and paid for by the State of Oregon upon authority of the governor's office. The detective section is under the command of a captain who supervises two lieutenants, twenty-five detectives and one stenographer. The work of this section is divided into two categories: (1) crimes against persons, and (2) crimes against property. Also two detectives are assigned to the district attorney's domestic relations staff and work full time on nonsupport and related cases.

The juvenile section was created shortly after the construction and opening of the county juvenile home in 1950. There are eight full time employees serving in this section, including a lieutenant in charge, four male deputies, two female deputies and one stenographer. The juvenile section is a specialized unit whose police personnel require special skills and abilities in handling and understanding the juvenile offender. These personnel handle about 2,500 cases annually, including all missing persons reports made to the Sheriff's police department.

Services Division

The services division is headed by a deputy chief and includes the following sections: (1) jails; (2) records and identification; and (3) scientific investigation.

The jail section includes all three jails supervised by the sheriff. These are jails at Rocky Butte, the courthouse, and Troutdale.

The personnel at Rocky Butte Jail include one captain who is in charge of all three jails, one lieutenant, three sergeants, twenty deputies, one chief clerk, five matrons, one steward and six civilian employees, a total of thirty-eight persons. Rocky Butte Jail was originally constructed with Federal WPA funds. After opening in 1941, an addition financed entirely by Multnomah County was opened in 1946. This institution is located just outside the eastern edge of Portland, about nine miles from the courthouse.

The jail has a maximum capacity of 400 prisoners and is rated as a maximum security institution. The average daily population is about 300 men and fifteen women. As there are no federal detention facilities in the Portland area, all federal prisoners, as well as those sentenced by the county and in some instances prisoners sentenced by the City of Portland, are held in this jail. Prisoners from other Oregon cities and counties and federal prisoners are boarded upon orders of the respective courts at two dollars per inmate per day. About 100 prisoners housed at the location are waiting trial on felony charges. The only other felons housed at Rocky Butte are those whose cases are being appealed or persons waiting transfer to the Oregon State Penitentiary or federal penitentiaries.

The courthouse jail is located on the seventh floor of the county courthouse in downtown Portland. It is supervised by one lieutenant in charge of thirteen deputies. Four of the deputies serve as court guards (bailiffs). This jail is essentially a holding facility for persons who are undergoing trial, being arraigned, or having prolonged appointments with defense attorneys.

The sheriff's third (and newest) jail is the Multnomah County Correctional Institution. It is a minimum security institution located in Troutdale, Oregon, about twenty miles east of downtown Portland. The paid staff consists of one lieutenant, one sergeant, one clinical psychologist, one jail steward and seven deputies. A jail chaplain also works with those inmates desiring religious counsel.

The correctional institution was opened on December 1, 1963. It has a maximum capacity of 150 inmates under a single bunking system. This number could be increased by the use of double bunks. At the present time the institution houses an average number of about seventy male inmates, most of whom work at the adjacent Multnomah County farm. The outdoor work on the farm is conducive to the rehabilitation of prisoners. Inmates housed at the correctional institution are those who have been thoroughly screened and classified as minimum security risks. These are the men judged most likely to benefit from a rehabilitation program.

The scientific investigation section consists of four identification technicians supervised by a lieutenant. This section assists the detective, juvenile and uniform sections in many criminal investigations such as burglaries, homicides, assaults, suicides and morals cases. The technicians use photography, charting and other scientific methods in acquiring and preserving physical evidence to be used in court in the prosecution of criminals. The lifting, processing and identification of latent fingerprints is a major function of this section. The section has a mobile laboratory containing equipment needed in almost any situation that might be faced in the field. Thanks to this mobility, personnel with a scientific background may examine physical evidence found at crime scenes and properly mark and preserve such evidence. These employees often testify before the grand jury and the courts as expert witnesses.

The records and identification section has charge of all written and identification records of the sheriff's office and is the central agency for records and communications. This includes receiving all incoming telephone calls and radio communications. This section maintains and operates a teletype which is connected to law enforcement and allied agencies in Oregon, Washington, Idaho and California.

The records and identification section is headed by a

captain who supervises three sergeants, ten deputies, five identification technicians, one identification clerk, five police record clerks and one stenographer clerk, a total of twenty-six employees. One sergeant is responsible for all police equipment while another handles all extradition and warrant matters.

Each year this section indexes and files about 20,000 criminal cases, processes about 25,000 traffic citations and approximately 3,500 persons are photographed and fingerprinted. The criminal files contain criminal records of 48,000 persons, about 75 per cent of whom are from the Portland area.

The foregoing is a sketch of the department which now will require all candidates for deputy positions to possess at least a four years college or university education, including a degree, at the time of appointment.

Chapter 3

THE LETTER OF REQUEST

The text of the letter sent on June 7, 1965, to the Civil Service Commission requesting the baccalaureate requirement is a recitation of the needs for police candidate qualifications, the logic involved, arguments against such a decision, and a statement which asserts it is more prudent for a police force to remain undermanned than to lower standards and staff with "bargain basement" type personnel. The request for the higher standard included thirty-six supporting citations drawn from recognized authorities in the field of police administration. The text of the request submitted on June 7 follows in the next several pages.

Mr. Owen J. Card, Secretary to the Civil Service Commission, was instrumental in expediting the letter:

Multnomah County Civil Service Commission
County Court House
Portland, Oregon

Attention: Mr. Owen J. Card, Secretary

Gentlemen:

This is an appeal for the establishment of a four-year college requirement for the job of Sheriff's Deputy in Multnomah County. It is not an ill-considered or rash move. It is a valid, proper and necessary objective—one that can and should be implemented now.

There are many factors to be considered, some more important than others. The sheriff's office has taken these factors into consideration and reached a decision. Another decision must now be reached by the Civil Service Commission. Also involved in that decision will be the police administrator's right to set standards for his department. What follows in these pages is intended to provide the Civil Service Commission with sufficient facts and data to reach an informed decision. We have attempted to be as brief as possible and do justice to the issues involved. Much is quoted from publications and from individuals whose words and reputations are respected throughout the police service in the United States and beyond. Some ideas and facts will be stated several times and in different ways, but all are important to the central question. The content as a whole, however, speaks directly to the issue and, to bring the subject home, will greatly influence law enforcement in Multnomah County from this day forward.

LAW ENFORCEMENT IN A DEMOCRACY

The police service of any nation forms a keystone in the structure of government, whether that government be a democracy or dictatorship. In the police state, the unrestrained and direct execution of centralized policy and rigid law results in an enforcement program which is most often arbitrary and cruel, and which most often disregards the dignity of its citizenry. In a democracy worthy of its name, compliance with governmental policy and law is effected by enforcement which is reasonable and which is dedicated to the protection and service of each individual citizen.

Police service is usually rendered by individual law enforcement officers in a person-to-person manner. The quality of that service, even though partially dependent on equipment and techniques, is ultimately dependent upon the individual police officer. Therefore, the competence, integrity and dedication of each officer is vital to the police service and contingent upon sound personnel management.

THE CURRENT SCENE

In 1957, Dr. A. C. Germann prepared a technical study for Saginaw, Michigan, which was attempting to determine whether or not Michigan's state civil service law, Public Act 78, was sound and suited to the needs of Saginaw's police personnel. In his essay, Dr. Germann discussed the need for police service and securing superior police personnel. He also summarized the state of policing in the United States, buttressing his contentions by citing from the writings of several leading authorities on American police organization and management. Dr. Germann wrote:[1]

"Crime rates are ascending. Since 1950, the population of the

[1]Dr. A. C. Germann, *A Study of "Act 78, Public Acts of 1935, Civil Service for Fire and/or Police Departments," as Relates to Police Personnel Administration in the City of Saginaw, Michigan, With a Survey of Alternative Devices, and With Recommendations for Change.* East Lansing, Michigan, August, 1957, pp. 61-66.

United States has increased 11 per cent and the volume of crime by 43 per cent."2

The traffic problem, the control of vice and juvenile delinquency, the protection of civil rights, increasing budgetary requirements, the depletion of manpower and a host of lesser issues plague the police administrator of today. Nonetheless, many of our police executives are meeting these problems with the same quality of manpower that was recruited at the turn of the century, myopically ignoring the real necessity for change in personnel philosophy and personnel management.

The American Bar Foundation, in its beginning research into the administration of criminal justice in the United States, note that:

> There can be no question that we have more and better police equipment in the United States than all the rest of the world combined, and this has been accomplished at no inconsiderable cost . . .
>
> Whether we shall face up to the hugh task of securing superior police personnel, not in a few jurisdictions only, but in all jurisdictions, and whether we shall pay for better police as cheerfully as we have paid for new police equipment remains to be seen . . .
>
> It is a notable fact . . . that the general pattern of American policing has undergone little change during the twelve decades that mark the modern police era.3

The problem of personnel is probably the most crucial issue facing the police service today. Apathy, indifference, inertia and the enervating effects of traditional police personnel policy are hurdles most difficult to vault. Yet, accent on the importance of police personnel management has been noted by every police commentator since the time of Sir Robert Peel. Part of this emphasis is due to the extremely sensitive nature of the police task. As one observer puts it:

> Policemen must make instantaneous decisions and these decisions may determine matters of life or death. At the least, those instantaneous decisions ordinarily affect matters of human safety or property rights or of personal liberty. In no other profession do mistakes in fact or judgment so frequently have an irreparable,

---

2Dr. Germann based his assertion on the publication *Crime in the United States: Uniform Crime Reports, 1957*. A review of *Uniform Crime Reports, 1964* reveals the trend to continue alarmingly upward; since 1958 the increase in crime has been almost six times greater than the population growth. Furthermore, between 1958 and 1964 inclusive population is up 10 per cent while crime is up 58 per cent. Dr. Germann's assertion of 1957 seems equally valid by 1964 standards. SGC & DEC.

3American Bar Foundation, *Administration of Criminal Justice in the United States*. Chicago, American Bar Foundation, 1955, pp. 77-78.

possibly fatal, effect. A physician may change his diagnosis, and a lawyer/may amend his pleadings. With the policeman, the die is cast when he makes his decision.[4]

It is precisely because the individual police officer has great discretion and, in many cases, several alternative solutions to the emergencies that he encounters, that he must be a highly motivated, carefully educated individual of great capacity.

The police budget is strained, the salary level low; the police task is ever more complex, and manpower in short supply. How do we provide effective police service with limited personnel? How do we select the most qualified? How do we develop our personnel to full potentiality? How do we provide motivation? How do we acquire effective compensation? How do we control personnel to prevent recurrences of those less salutary happenings, the history of which hangs as a millstone about the throat of today's officer? How do we eliminate the incompetent and immoral? How do we regain great losses of public confidence?

Improved fiscal administration, attention to planning and organization, inspired leadership, effective reporting and sound public relations will assist in the resolutions to these questions, but energetic attention to personnel management is an absolute essential to any fruitful and lasting solution.

Probably the most succinct and careful analysis available is that of Bruce Smith, Sr., speaking in England in 1954 on the American police service:

> The American people have been trying desperately for the last two or three decades to secure better police protection and a higher order of police service generally. Local political leadership has often misled them with the beguiling idea that they could have better police protection through the simple expedient of hiring more police and buying more equipment. As a result, our police quotas have shot up rapidly and we can boast more costly police equipment than all the rest of the world put together. Yet the goal seems as far removed as ever, largely because the standards for selection, promotion and discipline, as developed by our state and local civil service commissions have not produced a sufficient number of high quality recruits and superiors to deal effectively with the complex police problems of our time.[5]

Selection of Police Personnel

There is no more important phase of police personnel management

---

[4]Alfred T. Smalley, "Basic Police Practice and Procedure," *The Police Year-book, 1953.* Washington, D. C., The International Association of Chiefs of Police, 1953, p. 160.
[5]Bruce Smith, Sr., "Police Developments in the United States," *The Police College Magazine,* 3:227, Autumn, 1954.

than that of selection. It would be rare, indeed, that any line position—private or public—should command a greater degree of care and attention to the selection of its potential incumbent than does the position of policeman. And it would be rare, indeed, that any supervisory or executive positions—private or public—should command a greater degree of attention to the selection of their potential incumbents than do the demanding roles of police command positions.

PRECEDENTS THAT POINTED THE WAY

The following newspaper report recalled the pioneering efforts of August Vollmer to professionalize police services in Berkeley, California, while noting that Berkeley on November 14, 1960, raised its minimum educational entry standard to two years of college or university work:

The Berkeley Police Department, which forty years ago attracted world-wide attention with its elite corp of "college cops," took another step forward today and fulfilled the dream of its first chief.

It was in 1920 that Chief Vollmer, who later became known as the "father of modern scientific criminal investigation," conceived the theory that to professionalize the police service high caliber personnel with college educations were essential.

Chief A. H. Fording announced today that starting tomorrow applicants for positions as Berkeley police officers must have at least two years college education.

REQUIREMENT

The new requirement fulfills Vollmer's dream that all men on the BPD should have at least a partial college education. Berkeley now becomes one of the first departments in the nation to establish the requirement.

However, at the present time, more than 100 of the 155 men and women in the BPD have at least two years of college.

Vollmer's sturdy crew of officers got the title of "college cops" way back in 1916 when Vollmer—who already had startled the world of law enforcement with use of scientific investigation, the first fully-mechanized patrol and other innovations—fathered the first school of criminology at the University of California.

EDUCATION

Thoroughly convinced that a college education was essential, Vollmer instituted the practice of allowing officers to work at night and attend college days. Among the bright young men who took advantage of this were O. W. Wilson, (General) William Dean, George Brereton, Walter Gordon, John Larson and others.

One factor in establishing the new requirement, Fording said, is the increasing number of colleges offering a wider and wider variety of law enforcement courses and the larger number of students interested in the profession.[6]

In 1932, Chief Vollmer had retired as Berkeley chief, but he still entertained strong feelings about advanced schooling for officer candidates. In that year he wrote a letter to the city manager and city council:

The entrance standards for police vacancy applicants have been maintained, and we continue to recruit young men who appear to be especially fitted for police service. Every known scientific device is utilized to eliminate undesirable candidates, and should we fail to eliminate them by the methods used in the recruitment period, they are later eliminated by the acid test of closely supervised departmental work. A high standard of efficiency is required, and unless the individual can measure up to the established standard, separation from the service is demanded. By this rigid adherence to the recruitment plan, a police unit has been developed that is second to none.

The recruit training program continues, but it is evident that the time is rapidly approaching when the educational institutions of the state must take over the task of preparing professionally trained students for police service . . .

The police service has been completely revolutionized in the last few years, and an entirely different type of individual is needed. In addition to higher personal qualifications, there must also be added the professional training in order that the service may not be hampered and police candidates may be educationally equipped to perform the duties that are now assignable to policemen.

(signed) AUGUST VOLLMER
Chief of Police Retired

We are still approaching these goals set forth thirty-three years ago. Most will acknowledge that these goals have only gained in importance during these years.

O. W. Wilson, now Superintendent of the Chicago Police, wrote in the first edition of Municipal Police Administration *that:*

. . . twenty to thirty years ago the assumption that the average person had secured a high school education would not have been justified. The police department may legitimately match rising

---

[6]*The Berkeley Daily Gazette, 11:7, 8,* November 14, 1960.

standards of education with rising standards for police recruitment.[7]

*He recognized the rising standard of education among the general
populace and that police educational requirements should also
rise at least correspondingly.*

Wilson goes on to say that:

> Both education and intelligence of a superior quality are abso-
> lutely essential, intelligence being paramount. Figuratively
> speaking, you can't pour a quart of information into a pint recep-
> tacle—neither can you expect to get a quart of information, knowl-
> edge, comprehension or service out of a pint container.
>
> There are some observers who would require a college education
> as a prerequisite for a police applicant. The Berkeley, California,
> police department has recruited college graduates with some
> measure of success over a period of years. It is undoubtedly
> true that a university course has a real contribution to make to
> police work, and we may look forward to the day when police
> work has a wider appeal to college men. Until that time, how-
> ever, the requirement of education must be pitched at a lower
> level.[8]

These statements were made in 1938—twenty-seven years ago.

*The requirement of education, fortunately, need not be pitched at
a level lower than a four-year degree in Multnomah County in
1965.*

*This standard is attainable in sufficient quantity to fill the open-
ings that arise in the sheriff's office. This is a paramount consideration. The demands of turnover felt by larger departments
throughout the country often precludes the elevation of recruitment standards although they might wish to do so. Such is not the
case in Multnomah County. We need not accept less than applicants with a four-year degree.*

THE BERKELEY EXPERIMENT IN PERSPECTIVE

*A report dated May 10, 1963, from William Danielson, City of
Berkeley Personnel Director, to City Manager John D. Phillips
made the following observations:*

> The present standards of employment for the Berkeley Police
> Department (two years college) are necessary and essential.
> These standards have evolved through fifty years' experience
> with selection of Berkeley policemen.

---

[7]*Municipal Police Administration.* Chicago, The Institute for Training in
Municipal Administration, 1938, p. 93.
[8]*Loc. cit.*

Experience has shown that present standards cannot be lowered without seriously affecting the quality and quantity of performance of police service. The philosophy of superior service of the Berkeley Police Department is conditioned upon attracting the best available men to perform police duties. The police service that the people of Berkeley have known for many years has been achieved and maintained with considerable effort over a long period of time. The present high level of police service can easily be lost by permitting a reduction in standards of police selection.

It is probable that in the near future it may be necessary to increase further the standards for selection of Berkeley policemen. The increasing complexity and difficulty of the policeman's job in the years ahead will require policemen who can successfully cope with these problems.

There has been an increasing realization throughout the country that better qualified men are needed in the field of law enforcement. Standards of selection for law enforcement are being raised throughout the nation. A dramatic example of the need for better qualified candidates for law enforcement is the evolution of pre-service education in law enforcement at the junior college, state college and university levels in California. There are thirty-five junior colleges, four state colleges and two major universities which now offer degree programs in law enforcement.

The insistence on high standards of employment from the beginning of the Berkeley Police Department has been the single most important factor in developing and maintaining the high quality of service and efficiency of the Berkeley Police Department.

Chief Vollmer's vision of the changing nature of police work, of the necessity for higher personal qualifications for policemen which are required to meet the new police problems, and of the development throughout the state of degree programs in law enforcement has come to pass and is continuing.[9]

THE DIVIDENDS OF THE EXPERIMENT

Washington State University Professor Emeritus Dr. V. A. Leonard described the dividends of the higher standards experiment in Berkeley and other West Coast communities:

At the other end of the spectrum in police personnel administration is one American police department where it has proved more difficult to gain admission than it would be to register at West Point. The entrance standards were high, as exemplified by the fact that a university education or its equivalent was considered desirable, if not necessary before being admitted to the entrance examination room. Only a very superior type of individual could hope to qualify in this examination which required from two to

---

[9]John D. Phillips, *Recommendation for Special Salary Adjustment for Class of Policeman.* Berkeley, City Manager's Office, May 22, 1963, pp. 7-9.

three days. The results in this case speak for themselves. With this type of personnel, Chief August Vollmer was able to present to the citizens of Berkeley, California, the lowest crime and delinquency rates of any city in its population class in the United States (85,000 to 150,000). The odds under which he achieved this record are revealed by the fact that Berkeley is located in the center of a dense metropolitan area, immediately adjacent to Oakland, San Francisco, Emeryville and San Leandro, where it is exposed to unusual crime hazards. In addition, he developed a police system costing less per capita than in any other American city in Berkeley's population class; this, despite the fact that the salary scale for his officers was higher than could be found in any other comparable department.

It is little wonder that the Vollmer system of police administration, one of the major contributions of the century to crime control, attracted international attention. The Vollmer police system is complex and involves many factors, but leading them all in importance are the high entrance standards that were established to recruit into the department only those individuals possessing superior intelligence and ability.[10]

THE JOB: WHAT IT IS AND WHAT IT TAKES

Colonel David A. McCandless, Director of the Southern Police Institute, University of Louisville, Kentucky, commented on the nature of the police task and what it takes:

> The day has arrived when no police executive dares to place officers on the streets, or in cars, who are untrained for the jobs. No one will, or can, deny that these jobs are tough. Certainly no comparable body of men is faced with the complexities of everyday, routine assignments that the modern police officer is called upon to handle. The policeman must not only be physically fit and mentally alert, but he also must be intellectually equipped to make split-second decisions; and these decisions must be correct ones.

> Probably at no time in the history of policing are administrators faced with problems of as grave import as those of today. Major crime in post World War II years shows a steady increase. Delinquency among juveniles has reached startling proportions. Traffic in municipal and rural areas alike presents a problem of such magnitude that our best brains are being taxed to find a solution. Yet these, and many like problems, daily call for police action and initiative.

> Badly undermanned as are almost all departments, many police administrators believe that the greatest need in policing at the moment is not more men but better men. This belief in no manner discredits the fine work being done by many police officers today. It merely emphasizes the need for exceptional men; officers

---

[10]Dr. V. A. Leonard, *Police Organization and Management,* 2nd Ed. Brooklyn, The Foundation Press, Inc., 1964, pp. 93-94.

who are equipped with the "know-how" to cope with the difficult problems of the day.[11]

Multnomah County Sheriff Donald E. Clark made the following assertion about policemanship and policing:

Because of the nature of modern police, the officer can no longer perform his function and be basically dumb. He must have an understanding of the complicated laws which he is charged with enforcing. He must have an awareness of the interpretations the courts have given those complex laws. He must see them in the perspective of the history of Western man and his striving toward basic freedom. He should know that the Constitution of the United States stems not from a void, but is constructed on the foundations of a long history of men striving toward basic freedoms. . . . It is important that he know the contributions made by such people as Pericles, Justinian, Voltaire and many other notable historic personages who contributed to our modern philosophy of government and law. I think it most important that he understand the complicated sociological and anthropological factors in racial and cultural questions. He should have a basic understanding of how his government works, how it is subdivided and how it is based on a system of checks and balances. And, he should know his police heritage—of Peel, Vollmer and Wilson.

Today's policeman needs knowledge of why people behave as they do. It is important that he not only know that a child steals, but that he also know, or attempts to know, why he steals. This, of course, means that he needs some understanding the field of psychology. To avoid belaboring the point, I will sum up by saying that the policeman no longer can be an artisan of a trade but must be a social scientist.[12]

Dr. Leonard added some additional thoughts:

The highest degree of intelligence available is none too good for the trying tasks that daily confront every police officer. The organizational chain is no stronger than its weakest link, and the stupid, blundering individual, who by his acts can bring discredit upon an entire organization, becomes the public's measuring stick for the whole department. One inferior man who fails to rise to an emergency can ruin the reputation of an otherwise excellent police force.

Rapid and accurate thinking is an essential quality of the police officer. He must decide in split seconds matters that may affect his own life or that of several persons. He must reach decisions concerning the application of the law without delay, and he must make no errors in arriving at his decision because the public is

---

[11]David A. McCandless, "Police Training in Colleges and Universities," *The Police Yearbook, 1956.* Washington, D. C., The International Association of Chiefs of Police, 1956, p. 173.
[12]Donald E. Clark, "The Role of the Individual Officer in Building Public Support for Law Enforcement," *Police, 8*:77-78, July-August, 1964.

always the "second guesser." A New York City police officer made a decision on one occasion and it later took the State Supreme Court six months to decide whether he was right or wrong. His perceptive powers, his imagination, his ability to concentrate his attention upon the tasks that are before him, his memory—visual and auditory—and his reasoning and judgment must all be of the best; otherwise, the individual must fail when confronted with some of the crucial tests that are the lot of every police officer. Furthermore, a high order of intelligence is necessary if the new recruit is to absorb readily the material submitted in the training programs, preliminary, intermediate and advanced.

Police entrance standards must provide for the selection of men possessing a superior degree of intelligence in order to assure satisfactory performance in positions to which the candidate may later advance. The patrolman of today is the potential sergeant, lieutenant, captain or chief of police tomorrow. The influence, therefore, of recruiting norms upon administrative standards for years to come is readily apparent.[13]

Los Angeles Police Chief William Parker addressed the annual meeting of the International Association of Chiefs of Police in 1954. He commented about higher police standards:

There can be no question that the police field is one of the most complex in which any man may assume a position in an attempt to engage professionally in a field of endeavor. One of the great difficulties of the police field is that it does not lend itself to exact science.

One of the problems in the police field is that 90 per cent, in my opinion, of police activity deals in the field of human relations, a field which has not been clearly delineated by any scientific approach. With the population of the country increasing tremendously, which means greater density, with all of the conflicts that occur when people are placed close together, and with the technological advancements that we must be familiar with—even in our own department they are training men in nuclear physics so that they can be taught to utilize various instruments to measure radioactivity, to translate things that we didn't dream about two years ago—so all of these additional burdens are coming upon us. The day has long since left us when it is simply enough to put a badge upon a man, to garb him in a uniform and say, "Go out and be a policeman."

There has been great progress made in bringing along and elevating the professional status of the police field. Wherever that progress is made, the reflection is well, not only upon the organization involved, but upon all organizations in the police field, and a stimulus more or less spreads about to invite others to move into this sphere of elevating the police work into a professional status and level.

13Leonard, *Op. cit.,* p. 95.

But, certainly, we cannot hope to do our job well unless there is
adequate training. We do not attempt to select the skilled policeman in the civil service examination at all. It is our job to train
that individual, if he has the intellect that is adequate, to absorb
the type of training that he must have if he is to have the skills
as a policeman. The day of what we used to call "a good practical policeman," in my opinion, is history and a thing of the past.
There were many people in the past who thought a policeman
doesn't have to know too much, if he just has a sense of judgment, that he can sort of keep things on an even keel. But when
we have the technical, highly informed underworld, and when we
have crime increasing at four times the rate the population increases, the day will come, if there is an upheaval through this
increase of crime, that the finger will be pointed to no one but
the police.

Society is like humanity. They have a habit of blaming other
people for their failures, and they look for the scapegoat. If the
crime in your community comes to a level where it is a public
scandal, unless your public relations have been good, you will
be singled out as the police executive, as the man who is re-
sponsible.14

THE ROAD TO PROFESSIONALIZATION

*In 1957 Dr. A. C. Germann, then Professor of Police Adminis-
tration at Michigan State University, East Lansing, wrote:*

A high school education or its equivalent should be set as the
absolute minimum educational level for the American police
service, and steps should be taken to elevate educational requirements to that of a college degree.

The modern police task is complex and demanding, and can only
be discharged effectively by superior personnel. *There is actually as great a logic in requiring a college degree for the local
law enforcement officer as there is for the federal agent.*

The local officer is, first of all, a law enforcement generalist; he
must know federal law, state law, county and municipal law,
traffic law, criminal procedures and their applications in his
community. He makes crime scene investigations, interviews
witnesses and interrogates suspects; he must know the scientific applications of police techniques, and know the practical
applications of psychology. He is, in many instances, called
upon to make decisions of the greatest consequence without time
for lengthy deliberation or consultation; he must exercise good
judgment in deciding whether to warn, or to cite, or to arrest. He
is charged with the most delicate task of "preserving the peace"
and must take immediate steps to restore the peace whenever it
is disturbed; he must exercise the greatest tact and diplomacy if
he is to achieve his purpose and retain the confidence of the

14William H. Parker, "Education and Training," *The Police Yearbook, 1955,*
Washington, D. C., The International Association of Chiefs of Police, 1955,
pp. 180-181.

citizenry. No poorly educated, emotionally unstable, half-trained officer can meet these strains; he will falter, and the press will have one more example of police deficiency to parade before the public.

Calls for raising the educational requirements for policemen to an Associate of Arts degree (two years of college) or to a Baccalaureate degree (four years of college) would be supported by public administrators, the bar association, academicians, and citizens with little opposition; in all probability, the most strident voices against such a proposal would come from within the police service itself—a stern indictment of professional aspiration. Certainly a four-year *technical* education at college is not necessary for a young man who wishes a law enforcement career; he could learn the basic principles in a far shorter period. It is the *kind* of education that matters—for we need leadership of the highest type—and college graduates entering the police service should be broadly educated with perception, perspective and understanding obtained by courses in psychology, sociology, English, history, and philosophy.

There are now some twenty professional groups, all represented by national associations, which have set minimum academic requirements in order to improve the quality and economic status of their practitioners, in order to protect the public, and in order to enhance their professional status. Not only Law, Medicine, and the Ministry have high academic requirements—but also Architecture, Business, Chemistry, Dentistry, Design, Engineering, Forestry, Journalism, Library Science, Music, Nursing, Optometry, Pharmacy, Psychology, Public Health, Social Work, Teacher Education and Veterinary Medicine. This writer would like to think that the police service well deserves the dignity that such programs give.

It is interesting to note that, in the State of Michigan, the profession of Pharmacy has progressed in thirty years from no educational requirements to a six-year training program. To be a registered pharmacist prior to 1929, one could take the state board examination if he had had some drug store work to his credit; after 1929, two years of college were required, as well as two years of apprenticeship before eligibility for examination; after 1939, four years of college were required; after 1955, four years of college and one year of internship was demanded prior to examination; and by 1960, five years of college, followed by one year of internship will form basic requirements. Even more interesting to note is the fact that the strongest support for this upgrading has come from the practicing pharmacists of the state who clearly realize that the resulting status and dignity is shared by themselves, as well as by the newly admitted professionals.

It would seem that the police service, in its advance toward professional status, would do well to support the college programs in law enforcement, recruit their graduates with great zeal, and energetically assist, through all police groups and associations, to raise the educational requirements for the police service. If the recruit of today is the chief of police of tomorrow, his preparation must be of the finest—if tomorrow's chief is to be the finest.[15]

The issue is clearly stated by the Civil Service Assembly of the United States and Canada:

In a career service system it is necessary to select entrants with a view to promotion and to the level they may be expected ultimately to reach. *It is not enough to relate educational requirements only to those of the entrance position.*[16]

The Honorable Stephen P. Kennedy, when he was Commissioner of the New York City Police Department, offered a significant thought concerning the professionalization of law enforcement when he asserted:

Professionalization is not a goal easily reached. The need for professionalization must be recognized on two levels: within the police profession and outside it—the public as well as the police officer must appreciate our aims and support our efforts before we can be successful.[17]

Bernard C. Brannon, then police chief in Kansas City, Missouri, addressed the following remarks about police professionalization to the International Association of Chiefs of Police meeting in 1956:

We of the police category of law enforcement have often discussed the advantages of attaining a true professional status. The attainment of a true professional status is the direction we have all chosen to take, for the words themselves represent concisely and neatly the sum total of our group dreams and aspirations. They denote a level of achievement within the police field upon which rests the finest of public service, greater prestige for the whole, and the best of personal working conditions. How to induce a universally recognized professional status for policemen is the question still crying for answer.

One thing is certain—isolated police accomplishment in only a few of our cities or even states is not enough; true professionalization will elude us so long as we fail to make our gains a nation-wide affair.

For over twenty years I have given theoretical and practical attention and study to the plight of the policeman. During this time I have been privileged to look up from the quagmire of a

15Germann, *Op. cit.,* pp. 25-27.

16Civil Service Assembly of the United States and Canada, *Recruiting Applicants for the Public Service.* Chicago, Civil Service Assembly, 1942, p. 52.

17Stephen P. Kennedy, "Law Enforcement as a Profession," *The Police Yearbook, 1956.* Washington, D. C., The International Association of Chiefs of Police, 1956, p. 177.

patrolman's darkest days, and down from the complexities of chieftainship; I have felt the cold pinch of nearly starvation police wages to the warm feeling of being able to meet my creditors with not so barren purse; I have seen the chaos and demoralizing effect of partisan political interference in law enforcement, and the fine, constructive teamwork of a police administration unhampered in its progressive activities; I have walked the shaky bridge leading from the dungeon of discouragement and despair to the lofty tower of highest hope and exultation; and if there is any scene in the police picture that has escaped me, I do not know what it would be.

My conclusion has been and is now that the American policeman's greatest and straightest path of progress lies in preservice education and training.

The college student who selects a particular field of study does so for various reasons, but usually it is because he intends to use the knowledge gained as a means of livelihood. He is looking for a career. His entrance into the ranks of any true profession is made only with the ticket of admission purchased at the price of higher level study and preparation. Either his college degree itself, as in the teaching field, or a state supervised examination successfully passed are the ordinary methods of qualifying for the right to practice his profession. These licensing prerequisites are earmarks of the established professions because they spell out an extended period of specialized study and training needed to learn the methods of service and to develop the skills required by the practitioner.

Turn now to our self-proclaimed police profession. Unlike the other true professions, there is no insistence on a college degree in police studies. There is no insistence on any pre-employment police knowledge or experience. The new entrant to our police profession, with rare exceptions, is both inexperienced and uninitiated in the very challenging and difficult field of law enforcement. Even in the business and commercial world some specialized academic training or prior experience is a customary qualification for work of importance.

So we see that the practitioner of police law enforcement skips the college level pretraining and study deemed so indispensable by all other true professions. Can he really do so and still lay claim to a professional status? Should the police profession itself assume the total obligation of training its own professional people after they have joined the police ranks? If so, when would the policeman really acquire sufficient knowledge and skill to validly claim a personal professional status? These questions should be faced.

Let us suppose that a salesman decided to become a medical man and went to a hospital where he received several weeks of training and then was proclaimed a doctor. If the authorities permitted this, there would be a public hue and cry of deafening proportions. To practice medicine without adequate knowledge, skill and experience is a dangerous evil. Our state governments recognized this long ago, and they did something about it.So did the medical profession itself. To become a medical doctor today, years of higher educational study are required by both the state and the profession. Since this is the only avenue of entrance into the medical field, the potential doctor eagerly submits to the prescribed training and study.

The days when the lawyer studied briefly in a law office and then became a member of the bar with full rights to practice is in the past. Our legal profession with the assistance of the state governments has raised its standards to the benefit of its members and the public. In varying degrees this is the case in most of the recognized professions. They invited state intervention when the protection of its citizens required it.

Any line of work which can adversely affect the health, safety or prosperity of the people, if improperly practiced or performed, should be subject to close scrutiny by the state. The quack doctor is no more a threat to society than the ignorant, imprudent or unskilled police officer.

Who is to honestly argue that our police work does not vitally affect our citizenry? Who is to urge with logic that it is not of professional caliber? I can think of no other line of human endeavor which requires the application of greater general and specific knowledge, skill and temperament. Our work borrows from all of the arts and sciences. It is certainly an indispensable type of service to the public and to the individuals, which is dangerous to all if improperly performed.[18]

THE FUNCTION AND IMPORTANCE OF A COLLEGE EDUCATION

The Honorable Quinn Tamm, Executive Director of the International Association of Chiefs of Police, Inc., editorialized:

Higher education is not a panacea for all of our ills. It offers, however, the most appropriate and adequate setting and resources for engaging in the search for better ways. Beyond the capability for conducting meaningful research and for enhancing our ability to objectively understand what is happening around us, the campus must be looked to for the police officers of the future. It is nonsense to state or to assume that the enforcement of the law is so simple a task that it can be done best by those unencumbered by an inquiring mind nurtured by a study of the liberal arts. The man who goes into our streets in hopes of regulating, directing or controlling human behavior must be armed with more than a gun and the ability to perform mechanical movements in response to a situation. Such men as these engage in the difficult, complex and important business of human behavior. Their intellectual armament—so long restricted to the minimum—must be no less than their physical prowess and protection.[19]

18Bernard C. Brannon, "The Set of the Sail," *The Police Yearbook, 1957,* Washington, D. C., The International Association of Chiefs of Police, 1957, pp. 17-21.
19Quinn Tamm, "A Change for the Better," *The Police Chief, 32:6,* May, 1965.

Mr. Richard Myren, Professor of Police Science at the University of Indiana, Bloomington, added his comments to a panel discussion about university training at the 1960 International Association of Chiefs of Police meeting:

Academic training has a truly different objective than the kind of training given in police academies. The academic viewpoint is that we don't believe we are training policemen, but we believe we are turning out the potential material from which policemen can be made. I don't think any university can train policemen. It is not a degree in policing that we are trying to give. The colleges and universities can give persons in law enforcement the orientation, the maturity and the powers of judgment which really count. This ability comes through the broad base of vicarious experience, for that is what education is—the beginning of vicarious experience. Anything that can be learned from experience can be taught from printed material. There is a difference in objectives and content of the program . . . . In-service training is mostly skilled training dealing with specific problems.[20]

Southern Police Institute Director McCandless made the following statement at the 1955 annual meeting of the International Association of Chiefs of Police:

One of the most significant advances in the police training field has been the emergence of the college and university programs, usually called either programs in Criminology or in Police Science and Administration. They are relatively new, although a few universities pioneered in their development more than two decades ago. In fact, the first undergraduate program is thought to have been started in 1916 at the University of California by the revered August Vollmer. This program became a part of the University's sessions and in 1950 was established as the School of Criminology. Recent advances in the college and university field have been substantial. In 1950 there were twenty colleges and universities offering programs of the preemployment type. By March, 1955, this number had grown to thirty-two, a 60 per cent increase.

I wish to make it plain that these programs are not meant to replace regular departmental training. In my opinion, when it is available basic police procedures should be handled, and can best be handled, by the department in its recruit training program. No college or university program should replace departmental training or on-the-job experience. The college and university programs are valuable supplements to departmental training and have a separate and distinct function. Each has a role in the training field.

---

[20]Richard Myren, "Need for Accelerated Progress in Training," *The Police Yearbook, 1961*. Washington, D. C., The International Association of Chiefs of Police, 1961, p. 195.

Preemployment Programs

The preemployment type programs are designed primarily to attract young high school graduates who desire a career in some aspect of criminology. The programs are usually divided into three main groupings: law enforcement, criminalistics and corrections. Several of the universities and colleges offer programs in all three divisions but the majority center on one or two of them. The tendency of all of them "is to raise police work from the level of a vocational occupation with primary emphasis on the physical and enforcement aspects, to that of a profession concerned with social forces, human motivation, and crime prevention."

. . . The great majority of these college trained officers receive assignments and have been of great value to the departments they have entered. Over the long pull, these officers will undoubtedly raise departmental standards and contribute in the march of policing toward professionalization.

Statistics kept by the colleges and universities show that graduates returning to their departments have a high promotion ratio and are being given greater responsibilities. The same statistics show that many graduates from small departments have returned to head up training bureaus in departments that previously had none.

College and university training, according to many chiefs with whom I have talked, has materially increased the operating efficiency of the officer upon his return. In most cases, he has acquired an increased morale and a greater belief in the dignity and "worthwhileness" of law enforcement as a career.[21]

University of Indiana Professor of Police Science Robert Borkenstein also spoke at the 1960 International Association of Chiefs of Police annual meeting:

My conception of preparatory university training is not to provide a license to enter law enforcement. Graduates of the police administration program in the various universities should not be considered "finished" police officers ready to go to work but, rather, as people who are inclined toward policing and who have a broad background that will increase their scope of knowledge and vision to take better advantage of the opportunities provided by the various police organizations. These preparatory courses in no way include preservice training which is so vital for every police agency to orient the individual.

We feel it is the university's role to bring into policing new ideas and new information from other disciplines, such as law, psychology, chemistry, sociology. This is why I have chosen to call university level training preparatory rather than preservice. Preservice training is the responsibility of the police organization

---

[21]McCandless, *Op. cit.,* pp. 173-76.

into which the individual enters.[22]

Colonel McCandless commented about the supply of college and university prepared candidates at the IACP annual meeting in 1955. His response in a sense responds to the inquiry raised by Multnomah County Civil Service Commissioner Harry White about recruiting base prospects:

The Supply of College Trained Candidates

The police science programs are attracting ambitious youth to law enforcement. This is shown by the steady increase in the programs of the preemployment type. As previously mentioned this increase has been 60 per cent in the past five years. My own experience and that of others in the training field emphasizes the point. During every week I receive three or four letters from high school students throughout the country asking what colleges and universities have courses in police training.[23]

At the 1964 annual IACP meeting in Louisville, Kentucky, Gene Muehleisen, Director of the California State Commission of Peace Officers Standards and Training, Sacramento, participated in a panel discussion about standards. His comments, reported below, also serve to respond to questions raised about recruiting base:

I would like to give you some statistics from the Bureau of Industrial Education. In its 1962-63 Fiscal Report in the State of California, they noted that there were 130 trade and technical courses, 130 offerings of some type where you could earn a degree.

Now, as you might guess, the course in Electronics Technician had the greatest number of enrollments, with 23,000 in that particular course.

But the thing that completely surprised not only the police community in our state (California) but also the educators, was the fact that the Number 2 program out of 130 programs was Police Science with 13,000 enrollments.

Now, what is happening on the educational level within California police agencies? Well, there's been a remarkable change in the past four or five years. It's been going up for ten years, but in the last four years it's jumped up rather dramatically.

If we were to combine our two largest police agencies in California, the Los Angeles Sheriff's Department and the Los Angeles Police Department, we'd find that their combined personnel is around 8,500 people, and their jurisdiction covers 3,682 square miles.

---

[22]Robert Borkenstein, "Progress in Police Training, A Workshop," *The Police Yearbook, 1961.* Washington, D. C., The International Association of Chiefs of Police, 1961, pp. 184-85.
[23]McCandless, *Op. cit.,* p. 175.

In there we find one Doctorate, thirty-four Master's degrees, ninety-five are engaged in graduate work toward their Master's degree. Fifteen with Law degrees, 464 Baccalaureate degrees, 641 Associate in Arts degrees, and over 65 per cent in those agencies have had at least one year of college.

And the most remarkable thing that I have noticed in the last class of Ed Toothman, Chief of Police of Oakland, California, is that there are twenty men in that basic recruitment class, and out of twenty men he's got fourteen with Bachelor degrees. We haven't seen anything like this in California to this day. He had three recruit classes in 1963 and they averaged two years of college per recruit class. We thought this was going to be the tops for a long time, but they have exceeded that and this is happening at various places throughout the state.

What about the agencies that require college education of some kind? We find that there are five in California that require two years of college as a minimum recruitment standard. In addition to these, there are eleven cities that require between one and two years of college.

And Walnut Creek, one of the smaller cities with twenty-six sworn personnel, that requires two years of college, also requires a Baccalaureate degree to be eligible to take the Sergeant's examination.

. . . It is too early to predict where we are going to level off in this matter of police education, or to estimate the sociological or the economic value of establishing professional standards for the selection and training of our peace officers.

However, I strongly join those of you who are of the opinion that our task is the most important function of government, that our job is so complex and so vital to our way of life that we must have the best-selected, the best-trained and the very best-educated people that we can get to do the job.

Well, now that we are going to this two-year requirement are we going to be able to get people to take the exam?

Chief Davis (El Monte, California) . . . got ninety-nine applicants with two years of college and in talking to these people (he) found that this competition interested them and the fact that they were going to an agency which had higher standards was of great interest to them.

There is a little department called Westminster in Southern California that has thirty sworn personnel. Every single man on that department is attending college. The scheduling is tough (but) the thing that amazes me is that they are doing a terrific job.[24]

The late Dr. Paul W. Tappan, Professor of Criminology at the

[24]Gene S. Muehleisen, "Mandatory Minimums or Professional Maximums," *The Police Yearbook, 1965.* Washington, D. C., The International Association of Chiefs of Police, 1965, pp. 313-17.

*University of California, Berkeley, at the time of his death, and
for a number of years associated with New York University, commented on the significant increase in standards in the police
service, especially in urban police departments:*

> In a considerable number of urban departments today a new tra-
> dition has been or is being established. The emphasis in these
> departments is upon securing men of fine intelligence, education
> and physical condition, providing salaries and promotional and
> retirement opportunities that are attractive to men of high calibre,
> and giving them training both in specialized skills and in human
> relations. There are at least twenty universities that now offer
> advanced programs of police training in various parts of the
> country, especially on the West Coast. More and more commonly
> we find officers with college, graduate, and law school degrees
> on metropolitan forces, pushing successfully for the profes-
> sionalization of police work and assuming leadership in their
> departments. In many cities these officers face great obstacles
> in the inertia of deeply rooted conservative practice. Yet the
> scene is shifting rapidly in important cities throughout the
> country. Such outstanding leaders as the late August Vollmer in
> California, "the nation's greatest cop," J. Edgar Hoover with his
> leadership in the Federal system, and Bruce Smith and Commis-
> sioner Kennedy in New York have done much in promoting ideal-
> ism and high standards of skill and honesty. These men bring
> fresh hope for effective performance in what, in terms of our
> ambivalent demands upon law enforcement activity, is one of the
> most difficult among our occupational specializations.[25]

Former Kansas City, Missouri, Chief Brannon added:

> We must have a greater objective, a greater goal, a greater con-
> sideration. The fact that we are going to have college-trained
> policemen some day doesn't reflect on the older men in the de-
> partment who have not had that advantage. Certainly there is no
> substitute for experience. And certainly none of us would trade
> some of our wise old heads who have been carrying the ball for
> us for some fresh kid just out of college with a doctor's degree in
> criminology. But we must remember there is a bumper crop of
> kids coming along. Our educational institutions are bursting at
> the seams now. There are going to be more and more properly
> trained professional people than there are places for in the
> various professions. We, as police administrators, must have our
> fair share of these college-educated people, and we must start
> now not only to train our present personnel, but to look to the
> needs of our future personnel.

> Certainly there is no status quo in our field. We must go forward
> on all fronts, and this applies definitely to the educational facets
> and ramifications. There is no more important consideration
> today than the education of our police personnel and the raising

---

[25]Dr. Paul A. Tappan, *Crime, Justice and Correction*. New York, McGraw-
Hill, 1960, pp. 312-13.

of our standards on every front and the specialization that must come if we are to have the kind of law enforcement we envision for the future.[26]

Professor Borkenstein of the University of Indiana argued that increasing standards in law enforcement was merely a matter of the police keeping pace with the public generally:

The other day I was interested in interpretation of intelligence tests in World War I and in World War II. I noted that a person who happened to be in the top 3 per cent in World War I dropped to the top 15 per cent in World War II. We don't know how much progress has been made since 1945, but this indicates our public is becoming more informed, more intelligent and more educated. For that reason law enforcement must necessarily keep pace.[27]

THE IMPACT OF HIGHER EDUCATION ON THE POLICE SERVICE

Professor Leonard had extensive comment about the impact of higher education on law enforcement:

It can now be said that more than 10 per cent of the total personnel in metropolitan police departments of the United States possess from one to four years or more of university training! This infiltration of university-trained men, although proceeding for the most part unnoticed, marks a significant turning point in American police history. The performance record of these men is paving the way for formal elevation of educational standards in the police service and has directed attention to the need for the establishment of professional curricula in universities and colleges affording specific training of men and women for entry into this branch of the public service.

. . . It is undoubtedly true that the complex nature of modern police service and the trend toward professionalization have operated as factors in challenging the interest of college-trained men and women. The presence of men with a university background is no doubt largely responsible for an ascending average intelligence level among the personnel of American police forces today.

Since, in American police service, administrative as well as supervisory and command positions are filled by promotion from the ranks, the implications of recruiting standards and procedure are self-evident. The application of university police training and research to the immediate problems of police administration can have far-reaching results in this important area of social control.

---

[26]Bernard Brannon, "Need for Accelerated Progress in Training," *The Police Yearbook, 1961.* Washington, D. C., The International Association of Chiefs of Police, 1961, pp. 190-91.

[27]Borkenstein, *Op. cit.,* p. 191.

Every major university and college already includes in its offerings more than 90 per cent of the subject materials that should be geared into a professional police curriculum leading to the Bachelor degree.

The application of university facilities for instruction and research to the immediate problems of police administration is a matter of considerable social significance. The impact of higher education on this branch of the public service can be understood to advantage in terms of the responsibilities of a modern police organization. Most of the arts and sciences are directly involved in the problems that confront modern police service and adequate preparation for a professional grade of work in this branch of the public service must of necessity include the study of academic subjects which bear upon police problems and their solution. Political science, public administration, sociology, psychology, biology, chemistry, physics and mathematics, among others, are basic artillery pieces of the modern police officer and are an essential part of his training for career service in the police field.

It is now evident that preparatory work in the social, biological, natural and physical sciences is essential to the caliber of police performance demanded by the dimensions of the police problem today. The implications of high level training for this branch of the public service in terms of sound public policy, lowered police costs and increased performance efficiency cannot escape the attention of municipal authorities and the taxpayer.

It has been stated that police service is an undertaking equally as technical as medicine, engineering, pharmacy, law and other professions and it follows that the only point at which men and women may prepare adequately for career service in this field is in the classrooms and laboratories of the university and college.

University training for the police services has long since passed beyond mere speculation. It is an established fact. Over one hundred universities and colleges now offer organized courses of instruction at the academic level in the law enforcement major, with from thirty-five to forty providing the opportunity for work toward the Bachelor degree in police science and administration, a substantial number offering in addition, the Master's degree, and two where the Ph.D. is available. The number is steadily increasing each year.

Today, with the ever-growing problem of reaching a compromise between a maximum of personal liberty and the restraints which must be imposed by a complex society, there is a special need for an understanding by future leaders of the role that law enforcement administration plays in our social structure.[28]

There is mounting evidence that advanced (beyond high school)

[28]Dr. V. A. Leonard, *Police Organization and Management,* 2nd Ed., Brooklyn, The Foundation Press, Inc., 1964, pp. 128-29.

education is considered essential for men who seek promotion within police forces. Such thinking is posited upon the premise that if duty performance at the entry level—the level of execution—is challenging and requires more than a high school diploma, in successive steps up the promotional ladder the man should be commensurately better educated. Noted police consultants Esther and George Eastman articulated such a proposal when they recommended the following in their 1962 survey of police organization and management of the St. Paul, Minnesota Police Department:[29]

RECOMMENDATION — 42.5

Patrolmen should not be appointed to the rank of sergeant until they have had one year of college work; two years should be required for promotion to lieutenant; three to captain; and four years to positions above this rank.

Failure to complete the required college work for promotion does not deny eligibility for the examinations if the work can be completed before the termination of the eligibility lists.

This requirement should be in recruiting announcements and in the basic manual so that all recruits will be fully aware of it.

It should not apply to men presently in the bureau. Instead, it would be well to give nominal credit to those presently in the bureau who have the initiative to pursue a college education. The latter provision would be established immediately and continue through the service of present employees.

George Eastman, former chief in both Seattle, Washington, and Pontiac, Michigan, and formerly a superintendent of the Port of New York Authority, also urged that the St. Paul Police Department request adequate funds from the city for creation of an educational refund program. Such a program would aid officers who chose to pursue advanced education by providing a degree of financial relief upon successful completion of courses:

RECOMMENDATION — 42.6

The bureau should establish an education refund program.

To encourage and to help policemen go to a college or university, financial assistance should be provided by the bureau. It is recommended, when a sworn member is pursuing a college program acceptable to the bureau, that he be required to pay his own tuition fees at the time of registration but on the successful completion of a course in an approved program he

---

[29]Esther and George D. Eastman, *Bureau of Police, St. Paul, Minnesota: A Study and Report*. East Lansing, Michigan, The Eastmans, 1962, pp. 128-29.

should be refunded one-half of his tuition fee.

RECOMMENDATION — 42.7

Grades below a C should not be considered in fulfillment of
RECOMMENDATION 42.5 above, nor should fees for such courses
be reimbursed.

> It is essential, in order to obtain maximum benefits from
> college programs that policemen students be required to main-
> tain acceptable college standards.[30]

THE CHOICE: MOVE BACKWARD, STAND PAT, OR MOVE AHEAD?

*The dimensions of the problem are commonly recognized. Why then
has not more and swifter progress toward true professionalization
been made? The foregoing material reveals, directly or indirectly,
many of the reasons. Others are implied.*

*Multnomah County has moved ahead and can be proud of its prog-
ress in raising recruitment standards and building a stronger and
more efficient police department. The task, however, is not complete nor should it ever be considered as completed. The fact
remains that further progress can be made and made now by raising
the educational level from two years of college to four years of
college. Our particular situation gives us advantages not enjoyed
by many departments. There is no reason to hold back. Why then
should we?*

EXPLORING THE ARGUMENTS

*Let us look at what we may call reasons for not further raising
educational requirements for deputy sheriff candidates in Multnomah County. Many of these arguments, it will be obvious, have
already been dealt with in one way or another and need no counter-
arguments here.*

1. *Other police agencies have the same or lower educational requirements.*
2. *The recruiting base is not adequate; Multnomah County cannot
   attract suitable candidates in sufficient numbers.*
3. *Raised standards would close employment opportunities to otherwise qualified applicants.*
4. *The public is not demanding higher recruitment standards.*
5. *Education is not a substitute for practical experience.*
6. *You cannot educate finished policemen, they must be trained.*

---

[30]*Loc. cit.*

7. *You do not need a college degree for police work.*
8. *Higher educational standards would result in an accelerated rate of turnover since deputies would be more inclined to leave for other police agencies or jobs outside the police service.*

Some of these arguments may make sense to some people. None will stand the test of close scrutiny. They are all answerable— logically, soundly and convincingly. In each instance the counter-argument far outweighs the superficial reasoning behind these arguments.

THOUGHTS RELATIVE TO ARGUMENTS

The statements and writings to follow have been selected to answer, in part, the arguments given above as reasons why Multnomah County should not raise the educational requirement for deputy sheriff. They touch briefly on many subjects. Their arrangement is haphazard; their logic is not.

Chief Brannon and Dr. Leonard spoke to several of the objections about elevating standards. Chief Brannon said in 1956:

> Some have reasoned that current police working conditions, longer hours and lower salaries than private industry, are large enough obstacles in the way of obtaining new police personnel. They say that if we add another barrier, such as preservice state examinations, the employment problem will become more acute. I have reminded them that there is no permanency to status quo; there must either be progression or regression in our push to better standards. If we make the acquisition of a police position too easy, we discourage incentive and invite inefficiency.

> Any move on our part that tends to make the attainment of the policeman role a more honorable and proud accomplishment will tend to attract more and better recruits, men of the kind and type we now seek with eagerness. The salubrious truth is that our working conditions have continually been on the upgrade, and this is because we have upgraded our profession.[31]

Dr. Leonard wrote the following:

> Admittedly, the person possessing an absorbing interest in the police service may be able to overcome intellectual defects; advocates of interest tests assert that a consuming interest in any field cannot fail to bring success to its possessor. It is extremely doubtful, however, that there ever was a successful policeman who was not unusually intelligent. In some positions a person with limited mental equipment who is greatly interested

---

[31]Brannon, "The Set of the Sail," *Op. cit.,* p. 23.

will make a good showing, but in the police service there appears to be a level beyond which a policeman cannot go unless he has superior mental equipment.[32]

California Commission on Peace Officers Standards and Training Director Muehleisen and E. Wilson "Bud" Purdy, formerly Chief of the St. Petersburg, Florida, Police and presently Commissioner of the Pennsylvania State Police offered answers to the arguments against improving standards. Mr. Muehleisen said:

I recall one area where there were four or five, a little cluster of police agencies involved, and a couple of the chiefs were against this type of program. They said, "Well as soon as they get these highly trained people working for me, they are going to leave. They are going to go to the highway patrol or someplace else."

And one of the chiefs in the group convinced all of them with, I think, some very simple logic. He said, "I would rather have on my department one good man for one year than a bum for twenty years."

When we talk about losing personnel, nobody ever talks about gaining these people. But they are moving around within our state . . . so somebody is gaining. Every time you lose one, somebody else is picking him up. But we never hear about that . . . .

The proselyter doesn't say much. But the fellow that loses a man says a great deal. So I don't think, when you look at it on the broad basis either statewide or even nationwide, that we are losing at all. We are really gaining.[33]

Commissioner Purdy added:

Most police administrators, particularly below the position of Chief, are promoted from the ranks. Because of this system, we, as Chiefs, are saddled with the extra burden of developing and educating administrative and supervisory personnel starting with the raw material pool at the patrolman level. Our organizations must be at the same time both active producers of a top quality product and educators of the producing personnel.

. . . Regarding education, a federal agent must be a college graduate. Yet, the municipal police service is far more complicated, technical, and of far greater importance to the American way of life than is the federal service.

Experience alone is not enough. Relied upon solely, it is the most expensive and inefficient teacher. The average police officer with twenty-five years of service may actually have one year of experience, twenty-five times. The officer who merely repeats his experience at the same level month after month and

---

[32]Leonard, *Op. cit.,* p. 94.
[33]Muehleisen, *Op. cit.,* p. 315.

year after year does not grow . . . and if he does not grow, he
cannot be equipped for serious consideration when an opportunity
for advancement occurs. This narrow mold of experience alone
throughout his long years of service will be the cause of his
rejection, his frustration, his justified resentment.

Hiring the unqualified is always a costly mistake. The easiest
time to get rid of unqualified personnel is before we hire them.
Never again do we have an opportunity. Seldom are we able to
separate an unqualified employee without public embarrassment.[34]

*Chief Brannon in 1960 offered some thoughts concerning the in-
crease in crime:*

More and more policemen and more and more penitentiaries is not
the answer to our crime problem. As our . . . Director of the FBI
pointed out today, crime has increased four times the rate of
population growth in the last twenty years or so. Projecting to
1975, the 176 million people in the United States today will increase by 45 million more. At the present rate of growth in crimi-
nality, it would not be fantastic to contemplate a statistical
growth of crime fifteen times the rate of growth of our population. This is a very appalling prospect.[35]

*In drawing to a conclusion, Superintendent Wilson, in 1952, when
he was Professor of Criminology at the University of California,
Berkeley, spoke about several aspects of recruiting:*

There is no valid reason why any police chief should not insist
on having the eligible list restricted to candidates of any designated minimum level of intelligence that he desires, regardless
of whether the list is prepared by a civil service agency or not.

Arguments that the individual candidate may make a good policemen, even though his intelligence is somewhat below average, or
that the psychiatrist is not infallible and, since the candidate has
not been guilty of some overt act that would demonstrate emo-
tional instability, he should not be rejected, or that the incident
that raises doubt as to the suitability of his character was committed in the past, perhaps as a youthful indiscretion, and should
not be held against him must be recognized as unsound. Granting
the possible truth of any one or all of these arguments, it is
better to err on the side of safety; the doubt should be resolved
in favor of police service.[36]

The public, in fact, is demanding higher educational standards.

34E. Wilson Purdy, "Administrative Action to Implement Selection and Training for Police Professionalization," *The Police Chief, 32:*16, May, 1965.
35Bernard Brannon, "Need for Accelerated Progress in Training," *The Police
Yearbook, 1961.* Washington, D. C., The International Association of Chiefs
of Police, 1961, p. 190.
36O. W. Wilson, "Problems in Police Personnel Administration," *The Police
Yearbook, 1953.* Washington, D. C., The International Association of Chiefs
of Police, 1953, pp. 191-92.

These demands may often be indirect and may come in a hundred different forms, but they are nonetheless cries for an increasingly better quality of law enforcement. The courts too have ruled in such a manner as to demand higher educational standards. The conclusion is inescapable. The direction is clear. The need is apparent. The time in Multnomah County is now. We must create a recruiting situation that enables us to build a police department that is hard to get on and easy to get off rather than easy to get in and hard to get off.

There is no substitute for professional caliber personnel in a law enforcement body. No matter how good the equipment or how large the force, to have a top organization you must have quality personnel. As Sheriff of Multnomah County, I would rather go shorthanded than to lower standards of personnel.

The concept of Civil Service, as I see it, is not to enable a maximum number of people to qualify for jobs on the public payroll, but to get the best people into available jobs. This we have attempted to do. This we must continue to do. I, therefore, request that the educational requirement for the job of Multnomah County Sheriff's Deputy be established as a Bachelor's degree.

Very truly yours,

Donald E. Clark, Sheriff

Chapter 4

THE PRESS

The local press, represented ably by two well-established daily newspapers, the *Oregonian* and the *Oregon Journal,* were not without comment to the sheriff's proposal. Editorially and actually both newspapers enthusiastically supported the program. There was some constructive spoofing, most significant of which was a cleverly-worded short editorial and a timely editorial cartoon which coincided with the department's annual inspection. The Letters to the Editors column, following the July 13 decision, included a nominal number of letters which sought to chide the standard. Pertinent newspaper accounts and editorial support appear in the following pages:

SHERIFF RAISES SIGHTS[1]

Taking note of court decisions calling for new standards of performance in law enforcement, FBI Director J. Edgar Hoover observed that "inadequate emphasis on the professionalization of law enforcement is one of our nation's critical shortcomings in the fight against crime . . . Law enforcement must raise its sights, broaden its outlook, and insist on a higher caliber of performance."

Oregonians need look no farther than Multnomah County to witness the van of the response to Mr. Hoover. Sheriff Donald E. Clark has proposed to the Multnomah County Civil Service Commission that it raise the minimum educational standard for deputy sheriffs to a four-year college degree. His case is supported by a brief suggesting that the county would be the first in the nation to set such a professional threshold.

Currently the educational standard for a deputy is two years of college, as it is in most sizable local police departments, although most Multnomah deputy sheriffs have a college degree.

Lawrence A. Aschenbrenner, Oregon's state public defender, reflects the view of a post-graduate profession, the law, in his view: "Surely every police officer in whose hands society puts its very collective life should have a college degree."

District Attorney George Van Hoomissen is on record as favoring elevation of the minimum college requirement to three years by

---

[1]*The Oregonian, 34:*1, July 1, 1965.

1968, and a bachelor's degree by 1970.

Sheriff Clark says there is no need to delay, that there will be enough college graduate applicants to staff his department. For several years, national police leadership has recommended such an improvement in standards, dependent only on availability of qualified applicants.

Portland State College is among the institutions of higher education recognizing the need. The PSC administration has developed a four-year certificate program in law enforcement in conjunction with a bachelor's degree in an allied field—psychology, sociology, or political science.

Of course, a college diploma will work no magic in police work any more than it will in any other field. The point is to raise the sights of local law enforcement as J. Edgar Hoover and others have suggested—and thereby to raise the general level of performance. The County Civil Service Commission could set the pace for the rest of the nation by approving this request.

• • • •

CIVIL SERVICE TO REQUIRE BETTER EDUCATED DEPUTIES[2]

The Multnomah County Civil Service Commission Tuesday night made the county the first local police force in the nation to require deputy sheriffs to be college graduates with a bachelor of arts or bachelor of science degree.

Sheriff Donald E. Clark said that no other city, county or state in the country has this requirement.

The decision was made by Commissioners Donald C. Walker and S. Eugene Allen. Commissioner Harry E. White was absent.

Clark, a graduate of San Francisco State College, and his undersheriff, Samuel G. Chapman, a graduate of the University of California at Berkeley, said they have pressed for the college-degree-deputy-sheriff for three years. Clark took office in Jan., 1963. Chapman was professor of police administration at Michigan State University before he came to Portland.

Said Clark: "I'm very optimistic."

Said Chapman: "We'll make it."

Said Allen: "It's worth a try. I'm for it."

Said Walker: "I've always favored 'upgrading'."

A. E. McDaniels, president of Police Local Union 117, AFL-CIO, stood up in the Multnomah County Courthouse Room 680 and said he approved the commission's decision and congratulated Sheriff Clark.

Gov. Mark O. Hatfield, attending a Portland meeting with Evangelist Billy Graham, said he thought the county's plan was "excellent."

Hatfield said upgrading of police work must be accompanied by recruitment, training and "realistically backed up" with commensurate

---

[2]*The Oregonian,* 1:6-7, July 14, 1965.

salaries. The governor said the public must give full support to law enforcement to make any program work.

Commission Secretary Owen J. Card said the college degree requirement will become effective when the commission constructs the next deputy sheriff's list this fall, perhaps in November.

FIFTEEN COLLEGIANS ON STAFF

Chapman said the county now has fifteen college graduates on its staff of 210 "sworn members"—the sheriff's term for full-time sheriff's deputies and staff. The current pay scale, he said, ranges from $483 to $583 a month.

Clark said Multnomah County's deputy pay was third in the state following Oregon State Police and Portland Police Bureau. "We'll weed and screen," the sheriff said. "We need to be number one."

Clark told the commissioners he anticipates an increase in the number of applicants with college degrees, and that he believes the sheriff's office will continue to have a small turnover in personnel.

• • • •

DEGREE REQUIRED FOR NEW DEPUTIES HERE[3]

By JOE BERGER
Journal Staff Writer

The Multnomah County sheriff's office has become the first nonfederal law enforcement agency in the country to require that its new officers hold baccalaureate degrees.

The County Civil Service Commission approved the new standard for deputies Tuesday night in what Sheriff Donald Clark called a "landmark" decision.

The change was voted at Clark's urging. It applies to both male and female officers.

The commission also approved Clark's request to extend the probationary period for new deputies from six months to a year.

The sheriff's office in June, 1964, became the first in the nation to require a two-year college education for applicants. It remained, until Tuesday, the largest nonfederal agency with such a requirement.

Clark said the move is "in keeping with the times and recent Supreme Court decisions." He said he expects other agencies throughout the country to follow suit.

"Multnomah County can be proud that we are doing some pioneering. I would like to compliment the commission on taking a very progressive step," the sheriff said.

Clark said the change will not affect present employes. "Of course, we always have encouraged our employes to further their education in any way possible," he added.

---

[3]*The Oregon Journal*, 7:1-2, July 14, 1965.

Only fifteen of the 210 employes now hold bachelor's degrees or higher. Clark has a bachelor's degree.

The sheriff said the new requirement should boost the crime prevention capability of his office.

"This is an area where we are not now doing an adequate job— and we know it," he remarked. "But sometimes we are so tied up with other things that we just don't have time."

He said college graduates who like police work "will go where they feel their education will be used to advantage."

The sheriff said he will ask the County Commission for an increase of approximately $100 a month in deputies' salaries. They now start at $483 a month and receive $583 after five years. Clark said he will seek a starting salary of $569, with a maximum of $689.

Civil Service Commissioner S. Eugene Allen also supported a salary increase. "If we are to increase standards and make our officers invest more in their education, sooner or later it's going to cost us," he said.

Clark pointed out that both the Oregon state police and the Portland Police Bureau have a higher pay scale for patrolmen.

• • • •

WHERSDA FIRE, MAC?[4]

When, through the process of attrition, only college graduates will be serving as sheriff's deputies in Multnomah County, will their manner of address to the public be changed?

For instance, will a traffic deputy speak somewhat like this to a motorist stopped for speeding: "May I inquire, sir, the reason for your haste? Could you apprise me, please, as to the situs of the conflagration which appears to demand your urgent attention?"

One doubts such language will be used much, at least not after a few incidents of public incomprehension. You could make a taxpayer angry talking to him like that.

• • • •

FOR BETTER-TRAINED POLICE[5]

The decision of Multnomah County Sheriff Donald Clark to require hereafter that new deputies must be college graduates was bound to be made somewhere soon, by some police department.

Sheriff Clark deserves credit for taking the initiative here, and the Multnomah County Civil Service Commission is to be commended for backing him up by adopting the requirement. Multnomah County's is the first police department in the country below the federal level to make such a rule.

4*The Oregonian, 22:*2, July 19, 1965.
5*The Oregon Journal, 10:*1-2, July 21, 1965.

STANDING INSPECTION[6]

But others are bound to follow. No one needs to be told these days that crime is becoming more widespread, its causes more complicated, its perpetrators in many cases more sophisticated. It only makes sense for society to protect itself with the smartest, best-trained officers it can get.

The new requirement does not specify that the degree must be in police science or criminology. Any college bachelor's degree qualifies.

[6]*The Oregonian*, 22:3-5, July 19, 1965.

This is reasonable enough, at least for a start. For one thing, there are not many four-year college courses in police work anywhere in the country, and there are not yet in Oregon, although Portland State's authorities have approved the idea of starting one and the decision now is up to the State Board of Higher Education.

For another thing, college-level police training courses are not narrowly vocational. Rather, they usually include large doses of such subjects as political science, psychology, sociology, English and public speaking. The object is to broaden the mind of the prospective officer, not narrow it, and to this end the study of a wide range of subjects is necessary.

One suspects that one of the effects of bringing more college graduates into police work will be to raise the morale as well as the standards of the service. When an officer refers to himself as the "town clown," as we heard one do once in a small place in Idaho, he seems unlikely to serve either himself or his city well. The experience of successfully meeting the demands of four years of college ought to strengthen a man's self-respect.

As we have said before, a college diploma is no guarantee that its owner will succeed in the difficult, demanding field of police work. But the experience of many professions, from medicine and law to teaching and journalism, has been that the levels of achievement have tended to rise as the educational requirements for admission have gone up.

● ● ● ●

Chapter 5

LEGISLATIVE SUPPORT

There was legislative support for such a decision as rendered on July 13, 1965. But it dates to February, 1961, when House Joint Resolution Number 17 was introduced by Oregon State Representatives George Van Hoomissen (currently Multnomah County District Attorney), Robert Chappel, Edward W. Elder and Philip D. Lang during the fifty-first legislative assembly, regular session of the Oregon legislature. This was a resolution which called for higher standards in the police service and concluded by resolving that the Oregon State Board of Higher Education be asked to provide more training for persons presently serving in or those anticipating a career as law enforcement officers. While the resolution did not directly influence the Multnomah County Sheriff and the Civil Service Commission in the request and decision leading to the Baccalaureate degree requirement, it is representative of the progressive thinking which pervades countless governmental officials at local, county and state level in Oregon. The text of House Joint Resolution 17 as read on February 15, 1961, follows:

Whereas all the organizations in the State of Oregon, which are composed of law enforcement officers, have among their purposes the desire to create a professional status for men and women so engaged through pre-service training on a college level; and

Whereas the goal of every progressive law enforcement agency is to develop and maintain the most efficient service possible through better selection of pretrained recruits where they are available; and

Whereas the late August Vollmer, well known as the dean of law enforcement officers striving to place this service on a professional status, made this recommendation: "To establish and maintain higher standards of educational, mental, moral and physical requirements for applicants by establishing preparatory and promotional courses for officers in colleges and universities;" and

Whereas J. Edgar Hoover has stated that "The efficiency of law enforcement today is commensurate with the degree of training of its officers and only through modern police training can we keep abreast of the times in the increasing fight against lawlessness;" and

Whereas law enforcement has become an intricate, involved and comprehensive field and the various phases of such involving administration, patrol,

52

traffic, identification, laboratory, vice, juvenile activities, investigations, records, and communications can be better accomplished by personnel with preservice training such as is mandatory in the practice of any profession; and

Whereas common sense dictates that a person is no more qualified to enforce our complex laws without a professional education than is a person without a professional education qualified to practice the accepted professions; and

Whereas the protection of life and property in an efficient manner is just as important in the smaller community as it is in the larger community, because the officer in the smaller community will be called upon to act in many more diverse capacities, which, as in the larger community, may have a direct impact and effect in the economic, social and financial welfare there; and

Whereas most persons engaged in nonprofessional public services, such as barbers, beauty operators, salesmen, and many others, now by statute must meet certain minimum preservice educational and training standards, while none such are required for law enforcement officials by statute, or otherwise, except in and by individual law enforcement agencies; and

Whereas there are now at least eight colleges and universities in the United States that offer two to four year courses in Police Administration and Police Science, none of which are in Oregon, and only one in the Pacific Northwest, located at Washington State University, with approximately forty such schools at the junior college, state college and university level in the State of California; and

Whereas surveys made with high school graduates indicate that in the State of Oregon there are many young men and women who are interested in a law enforcement career, and who are desirous, upon graduation of taking college work toward such an end; and

Whereas such a group of graduates in the study of Police Science and Police Administration would provide an excellent pool from which to draw recruits for law enforcement agencies within the State of Oregon; now, therefore,

Be It Resolved by the House of Representatives of the State of Oregon, the Senate jointly concurring:

(1) The State Board of Higher Education is respectfully requested to assist in increasing the efficiency of law enforcement by offering this training to those qualified persons desirous of entering, as a career, the profession of law enforcement, through the study of courses to that end which courses with competent instructors are readily available.

(2) This resolution shall be sent to the Oregon State Board of Higher Education.

* * * *

Higher education in Oregon has reached a point where a four-year curriculum leading to a degree in law enforcement will soon be implemented. Dr. Branford P. Millar, President of Portland State College, reported on progress in a letter of May 28, 1965, to Sheriff Clark:

Portland State College is concerned with the training of prospective police officers to the extent that we have formulated a four-year certificate program in law enforcement. In conjunction with the certificate program, a baccalaureate program in an allied field (i.e., Psychology, Sociology, or Political Science) has been designed.

This program has been approved by the Portland State College Curriculum Committee and Faculty Senate; it will now go forward for approval by the State Board of Higher Education. We plan for the program to be undertaken as soon as funds are available and suitable arrangements made. The program has been designed along lines developed during extensive discussions with local law enforcement officials and after review of national practices.

This program in law enforcement is specifically designed for those students who desire a general, well-rounded background in the basic liberal arts leading to a Bachelor of Science degree in Sociology, Psychology, or Political Science with a certificate in Law Enforcement. It has been devised with the graduation requirements for a Bachelor of Science degree at Portland State College according to the current Portland State College catalog, 1964-65.

A degree candidate must complete a total of not less than 186 term hours. Other specific requirements are the following:

1. Upper division: minimum 62 term hours.

2. Work in residence: of the final 60 hours offered for graduation for any degree, 45 hours must be residence credit hours.

3. Correspondence study: maximum applicable to degree requirements: 60 term hours.

4. Grade-point average: minimum, 2.00 over-all, with minimum of 2.00 on all PSC work.

5. Non-major requirements: a minimum of 63 term hours, selected from approved courses (including General Studies courses) in the Divisions of Humanities, Science and Social Science, outside of the major department, distributed as follows:

   A. A minimum of 18 term hours of work in each division. These hours must include a 100 or 200 level sequence plus 9 term hours in each division. Of the latter, 9 term hours are to be in 300 or 400 level courses outside the student's major-division.

   B. In addition to (A) above, 9 term hours of 300 or 400 level *courses in any one division, or General Studies courses in any division.*

For the Bachelor of Science degree, 36 term hours chosen in either the Division of Science or the Division of Social Science.

In preparing this program of studies one of the fundamental principles that has been followed is that the student will receive the broadest possible training in the areas of the social sciences and sciences compatible with the degree requirements mentioned above and the postulate that a police or correctional officer in modern society should have a broad background in order to qualify him in the extremely complex role that these professions entail. Also a guiding principle has been the idea that professional courses in police or correctional work will be reduced to a minimum compatible with the premise that some professional training, especially of the broad-gauge nature, should be included in such a certificate program. It is suggested that the more narrowly based and more highly specialized police and correctional courses can best be taught by the particular organization wherein the Law Enforcement candidate finds employment after graduation.

We sincerely hope that all the efforts of educational institutions, law enforcement agencies, and civic organizations will be successful in raising the standards of law enforcement officials.

A recommendation in *Justice, the 1961 Commission on Civil Rights Report* urges Congress to offer grants-in-aid to promote professional quality of state and local police:

> Recommendation I. That Congress consider the advisability of enacting a program of grants-in-aid to assist State and local governments, upon their request, to increase the professional quality of their police forces. Such grants-in-aid might apply to the development and maintenance of (1) recruit selection tests and standards; (2) training programs in scientific crime detection; (3) training programs in constitutional rights and human relations; (4) college level schools of police administration; and (5) scholarship programs that assist policemen to receive training in schools of police administration.[1]

Perhaps the fruits growing out of the Law Enforcement Assistance Act, Public Law 89-197, signed into law by President Lyndon B. Johnson on September 22, 1965, will relate to those which the Commission on Civil Rights proposed. There seems

---

[1]*Justice: Book 5 of the United States Commission on Civil Rights Report*, Washington, D. C., U. S. Government Printing Office, 1961, p. 112.

to be a likely prospect that this will be so. When signing the
Act into law, President Johnson said the following:

Our efforts against crime must not, however, be limited to developing long-
range programs. We must also take prompt, direct action to halt the immediate
suffering which lawlessness brings to our citizens. It is my devout hope that
the Law Enforcement Assistance Act I have signed today will give us the
means to accelerate the fight against crime now.

This Act will make funds available to States, localities, and private organizations to improve methods of law enforcement, court administration, and
prison operation. For years, we have provided Federal assistance in the
fields of housing, employment, mental health, education, transportation, and
welfare. Because the anchor of society must be an abiding respect for law
and order, it is appropriate that the Federal Government provide material aid
to resist crime and promote the rule of law on the local level.

We are not dealing here in subsidies. The basic responsibility for dealing
with local crime and criminals is, must be, and remains local. But the Federal Government can provide an infusion of ideas and support for research,
for experiments, for new programs.

The policeman is the frontline soldier in our war against crime.

He bears a burden which increases each day. We must give him modern training, organization, and equipment if he is to succeed in saving our cities
from the malignancy of crime. This is a major objective of the Law Enforcement Assistance Act.

We recognize that speedy justice is both an essential of fairness and a meaningful deterrent to crime; yet we have permitted our criminal courts to flounder
in delay, lack of dignity, and the tortuous disposition of criminal cases.
Swift, fair, and effective justice is an objective of the Law Enforcement
Assistance Act.

We believe rehabilitation is indispensable if we are to break the cycle of
crime by convicted offenders. Yet, too often, we offer only four walls of a
prison containing no opportunity for learning a trade, maintaining family ties,
or preparing to return to the community. Too often prisoners do not leave
their confinement as law-abiding men. They leave, rather, as released criminals. Rehabilitation is an objective of the Law Enforcement Assistance Act.

These are necessary goals. But it is not enough to appoint a crime commission. It is not enough to sign a Law Enforcement Assistance Act. We must
move forward with the same commitment and conviction we have given our
attack on every other social evil that besets our people.

The local policemen, the local district attorneys, city and State judges can
know this President will support them, without hesitation, in their efforts to
fight crime in their towns.

I will not be satisfied until every woman and child in this Nation can walk
any street, enjoy any park, drive on any highway, and live in any community
at any time of the day or night without fear of being harmed.

I have directed the Attorney General of the United States to prepare a legislative program with this objective:

To strengthen the partnership of the Federal Government with our States and

local communities in performing the first and most basic function of government—the preservation of law and order and the protection of every citizen.

Chapter 6

EDUCATION IN ENGLAND AND WALES

On July 14, 1964, the London (England) *Times* quoted English Lord Gardiner as having said, "We are getting to a point where there are, I suspect, more university graduates among the criminals than there are among the police." The irony of Lord Gardiner's remarks emerges when one reviews a recent assessment of educational achievement of British policemen as reported in 1960 and 1962 by the Royal Commission on the Police. Though rather lengthy, citations from both reports express strong British resolve that the police service shall improve through attracting better-educated candidates. It also discloses that the British will promote the continued general education of young constables; improve the service's career potential to attract better-educated persons to the police; reduce the period of service required before a man is eligible to become a sergeant; and improve pay and training arrangements in order to compete at the manpower marketplace and secure a sufficient number of college-educated, career-oriented constables.

A table, "Educational Attainment of Recruits, 1959," which appears on page 27 of the *Interim Report, 1960,* introduces the English term, "General Certificate of Education (GCE)." *Whitaker's Almanack* explains the GCE:

Pupils in Secondary Schools (youngsters of approximately fifteen to sixteen years old) may sit for the examinations leading to the award of the General Certificate of Education. The nine examining bodies set papers at three levels, ordinary, advanced and special. Entrance to the Universities and to many courses of professional training depends on the results in these examinations. In accordance with the Third Report of the Secondary School Examinations Council a new and uniform system of grading and presentation of results of GCE examinations at A level will be used by all examining bodies. There will be five grades of pass awards on main or "basic" papers and two "supplementary" gradings (Distinction and Merit) for abler candidates who take B papers in addition to main papers: the existing Scholarship papers will be discontinued. In the summer of 1962 there were 37,000 candidates at Ordinary level; 1,140 at Advanced from modern and all age schools;

172,000 0 and 51,000 A from grammar schools and from other secondary schools 50,000 0 and 6,400 A.

The following excerpt from *Pears Cyclopaedia* reports:

Some examinations are normally taken while at school; others, normally only after leaving. The commonest In-School examination is of course the General Certificate of Education, though it can also be taken by those who have left school particularly in Technical or Further Education Colleges but also through correspondence.

UNIVERSITY DEGREE

The General Certificate of Education is essential for anyone wishing to take a degree at a British University, and the details for qualifying for University entry are uniform, except that Oxford and Cambridge are law unto themselves and every Faculty of each University has its own special requirements concerning particular subjects passed at Advanced and Ordinary level which is only to be expected.

It is readily observed that the English GCE concept is not easily equated with standard American primary and secondary schooling designations. Nevertheless, these descriptions of the GCE concept will better facilitate comprehension of material presented subsequently from the Royal Commission reports.

The following citations are from the *Royal Commission on the Police, 1960, Interim Report:*[1]

Standard of recruitment

81. The qualifications for entry to the police service are laid down in the Police Regulations, but the Regulations allow some latitude in their local application. A candidate for the service must be between 19 and 30. He must attain a minimum educational standard; he must be at least 5 ft. 8 ins., physically fit and possess a satisfactory health record; and he must be of good character and background and possess the right personal qualities.

82. Hence a police recruit must satisfy three requirements: he must be a man of integrity; he must be mentally and physically fit; and his education must be adequate. It would in our view be wrong to set any one of these above the rest, since all three are essential.

Educational standards

83. Entry to the police service is not regulated by any national examination: each police force conducts its own educational tests. The evidence about the educational standards demanded of recruits at the present day is conflicting. Some of the police witnesses contended that they have been lowered in order to meet the need for more recruits, but the chief constables did not accept this. Witnesses from the Home Departments also said that they were satisfied with the general level of educational attainment, although they and the local authority associations expressed concern about the shortage of outstandingly able entrants to the police service.

---

[1]*Royal Commission on the Police, 1960, Interim Report.* London, Her Majesty's Stationery Office, November, 1960, pp. 26-29.

84. It is difficult to draw any firm conclusion from these conflicting opinions. Nor was the statistical evidence available to us as helpful as we could have wished. We were supplied by the Association of Chief Police Officers with information about the type of education received by men recruited in England and Wales during 1959. This showed that rather more than 40 per cent of all recruits were educated at grammar schools or their equivalent (38.5 per cent in the Metropolitan force and 50 per cent in the City of London force). Information compiled on a slightly different basis by the Home Office showed that in England and Wales ex-grammar school boys form a substantially higher proportion of recruits with previous service as cadets (52 per cent) than those who join as policemen in the ordinary way (38 per cent).[20] Thus two out of every five recruits who join the service in the ordinary way at 19 plus and half of those who join from cadet forces have attended grammar schools. This compares with the national average of about one boy in three attending grammar or public schools or their equivalents.

85. It is necessary, however, to consider what standard of educational attainment these recruits have reached. We have compiled the following table from information supplied to us by the Home Office:

EDUCATIONAL ATTAINMENT OF RECRUITS, 1959

Percentages of Total Recruits with Recognized Educational Modifications

	1-4 GCE Subjects at Ordinary Level (1)	5 or More GCE Subjects at Ordinary Level (2)	2 or More GCE Subjects at Advanced Level (3)
	Per cent	Per cent.	Per cent.
Provincial police forces:			
ordinary entry	20	11	1
cadet entry	39	10	-----
Metropolitan police force:			
ordinary entry	18	11	2.5
cadet entry	40	20	2

86. These figures, in our opinion, give some ground for concern, and that concern is deepened if account is taken of much less favourable figures submitted by the County Councils Association which are based on the 1955-59 recruitment of 21 county forces covering a total population of 15 million.[22] It is unfortunate that we cannot break up the large group in column (1) of the table in the preceding paragraph into its components, for the difference between securing four passes and only one is great. It is, however, a fair conclusion that while the police service attracts a substantial number of grammar school boys, most of them belong to the lower half of those who leave the grammar school at 16. Apart from the London cadets, only one recruit in ten secured the five or more GCE passes at ordinary level which constitute a minimum professional entrance qualification, while over the twenty-one county forces surveyed only one police entrant in eleven had the four ordinary level passes demanded for admission to training for a considerable range of subprofessional occupations.

87. The intake of recruits with two or more GCE passes at advanced level is meagre indeed,[23] and we have come across no recent instance of a university graduate entering the service.

88. Here it is necessary to refer to a fundamental and long-standing principle of recruitment policy in the police service, namely that of appointing men only in the basic rank of constable. Unlike the armed services of the Crown and many civilian occupations, the police service has for many years filled the highest posts from its own ranks. "Officer entry" does not exist. We were assured by the police witnesses that the principle of finding future leaders from within the service commends itself to all ranks of the police. On the other hand, the County Councils Association suggested that, to enable the service to take its share of recruits of high educational standard, provision should be made both for graduate entry to, and for graduation during, police service, and that officers so qualified should have an early opportunity of competing on merit with other serving policemen for entry to a category of officers selected for accelerated promotion. In addition the Association recommended that some immediate monetary reward might be given to police recruits with high educational qualifications. The Association of Municipal Corporations invited us for similar reasons to recommend that police authorities in England and Wales should carry out an enquiry into methods of recruiting potential senior officers.

89. We understand, however, that the Home Office have under review, in consultation with the police and local authority associations, the closely related question of providing means of accelerated promotion for able recruits. These proposals had, unfortunately, not reached a sufficiently advanced stage for us to be able to study them at the time of our present enquiries. We are not, therefore, concerned at present to pass judgment on the basis of police recruitment, but we must stress that neither the existing recruitment policy nor any other can be considered fully satisfactory unless it meets two distinct requirements: first, that it secure an adequate number of competent policemen, and second, that it attract sufficient young men of such ability and educational attainments as will fit them to occupy in due course the highest posts in the service.

90. We cannot, on the scanty and sometimes conflicting evidence at present available to us, attempt to answer the question, what sort of education and standard of attainment should the policeman have? For underlying this question is another, more fundamental: what kind of policeman do we want in the latter half of the 20th century? This is a subject of great public importance which we must defer for our final report in the light of additional evidence which we shall receive, particularly about relations between the police and the public. Here it is enough to observe that the Desborough Committee in considering the pay of the constable dissociated him from the agricultural labourer and the unskilled worker, and gave him a social status which he has enjoyed for the past forty years—although the police maintain that this status has been lowered by failure since the war to maintain an adequate level of pay. We shall have more to say about these questions of social and economic status in our final report. And, in that much broader context, we shall return to the question of educational standards.

[20]In the Metropolitan force the difference is even more striking: 56 per cent of the recruits with cadet service have a grammar school education compared with only 30 per cent of other recruits.
[22]Minutes of Evidence 9, page 563. These figures showed that, in the 21 county forces surveyed, only 6.3 per cent of recruits during the last five years possessed the GCE with five or more subjects at ordinary level, 8.9 per cent had four or more subjects and 12.2 per cent had three or more subjects; 80 per cent of recruits did not possess the GCE at all. The Association said, however, that their statistics showed a slight improvement in the year 1959.
[23]Over the 21 county forces it is as low as one recruit in every 287.

The following pages are excerpted from the *Royal Commission on the Police, 1962, Final Report:*[2]

Educational qualifications of recruits

298. We said in our interim report that the available evidence on the educational quality of recruits to the police service gave some ground for concern; and we stressed that no recruitment policy could be deemed satisfactory unless (*a*) it secured an adequate number of efficient policemen, and, (*b*) it attracted sufficient young men of such ability and educational attainments as would fit them to occupy in due course the highest posts in the service. It is with the first of these requirements that we are concerned here.

299. To hope that improved pay and conditions will attract men of better educational standard is reasonable; but it would be unrealistic to expect that, if full employment continues, there will be a spectacular rise in the general quality of recruits, and irresponsible to propose for all entrants educational requirements so stringent that they must cause a crisis in recruitment. What makes it difficult to frame suitable educational tests for police entrants is less the fact that the majority of them have few if any passes in a recognised national examination than that nearly all of them have been away from school for anything from four to ten years.

300. We submit that the educational tests administered to police recruits should satisfy the three-fold condition that they are reasonably uniform for the country as a whole, that they are expertly conducted and that they are appropriate to the age and scholastic background of the candidates. In our view the existing practice fails on all three counts. The regulations lay down only that the applicant must "satisfy the chief constable that he is sufficiently educated by passing a written or oral examination in reading, writing and arithmetic", a form of words unchanged since 1921 and reflecting not unfairly the educational ideas of that date.

301. Obviously there cannot be uniformity of standard when, with no more guidance than this, some 150 chief constables are left with the responsibility for framing, marking and evaluating tests. Again, it is no disparagement of the able men who command our police forces to suggest that they are unlikely to be expert in the admittedly difficult art of the examiner. Thirdly, tests on the basic skills and the more elementary content of the curriculum, fairly reliable in assessing the attainments of young people at school, are wholly unsuitable for men from 19 to 30 years of age, for most of whom schooling ended at 15 or soon after. However skilfully such tests are made up and corrected, they can at best give some indication of the candidate's scholastic stock-in-trade at the time of testing, but they can tell little—and may easily mislead—about what should be the real concern of the authorities, namely the mental potential of the young men coming forward. If, therefore, the Police Federations, in calling for a national entrance examination, have in mind attainment tests of the traditional sort, it must be pointed out that such an examination would be of limited value and doubtful fairness, unless it was preceded by, say, a six months' refresher course in school subjects, a requirement which would adversely affect recruitment.

302. Our own recommendations seek, without derogating from the authority

---

[2]*Royal Commission on the Police, 1962, Final Report.* London, Her Majesty's Stationery Office, May, 1962, pp. 90-95.

and responsibility of chief officers, to bring an element of uniformity into the assessment of candidates and to ensure that in what is educationally complex expert educational advice is at the service of the authorities throughout.

303. We think that all candidates for admission to the police service should be required to take the same standardised tests. These, though including a vocabulary tests, would not be primarily tests of verbal ability but rather tests of the kind used for many years past on a very large scale in the selection of personnel by the Services, the Civil Service and industry. The validity of such tests as indicating where a given level of performance places the candidate within the general range of national intelligence has long been established and need not be argued here. It is worth remarking, however, that they have the further merit of largely ironing out differences resulting not from natural ability but from good or bad teaching, environmental variations, and length of time away from regular study.

304. Such test material would presumably be supplied by a body like the National Institute of Industrial Psychology to the Civil Service Commissioners, who would issue it to chief constables. A pass level would be fixed for the whole country, but while the attainment of this would normally be a condition of admission to the police service, it could hardly be made a requirement so absolute as never in any circumstances to be waived. It should be noted, however, that where recruitment was proving abnormally difficult, a chief constable would know at least how often and by how much he was being forced to depart from the approved standard of test performance. Moreover, as time passed and the test scores of all applicants were in the possession of the Home Departments, the authorities would know, as they have not known hitherto, just how well or how badly the police service was faring in the recruitment of ability relative to the distribution of intelligence in the distribution of intelligence in the nation as a whole.

305. Even now there must be few cases (and after a moderate degree of amalgamation of police forces there should be none) where the chief constable is not associated with a local authority which also has a chief education officer with a professional staff, and we urge that the co-operation of the experienced educational staff be sought to the fullest extent in this difficult business of judging the intellectual and educational calibre of police recruits.

306. To give precision to these general suggestions we recommend as follows:

(1) That the present regulation about the examination of recruits be rescinded.

(2) That the same standardised tests be given to all recruits.

(3) That a professionally qualified member of the chief education officer's staff give the standardised tests and report on them to the chief constable.

(4) That a short continuous composition on a subject within the candidate's range of experience and interests continue to be set in all cases, not however to assess writing, spelling or grammar, but to show whether the candidate can judge what is relevant and important in a statement. The educationist assisting the chief constable should mark the composition.

(5) That in the interviewing of candidates, the chief constable have with

him as an assessor the chief education officer or a senior member of his professional staff, or an experienced headmaster, to help in resolving such doubts and difficulties as must arise where the scholastic records of the majority of candidates have to be judged mainly or wholly from their school reports.

(6) That at some point in his probationary period the recruit be tested in the basic educational skills. To give such tests when a man seeks entry to the police service is ill-advised and often unfair. But once a candidate has been accepted, it would be wholly reasonable to point out to him that a good standard in writing, spelling, grammar, punctuation and arithmetic is essential in the job he has chosen; that he will be given guidance towards becoming more proficient in these skills; and that before the probationary period ends he will have to satisfy his chief officer as to his proficiency in them by passing tests. These tests should be set and marked by the Civil Service Commissioners.

(7) That, despite the heavy demands on police probationers, an effort be made to improve and extend their general education, either by having them share in the work of day-release groups or by the provision for them of classes arranged specially to meet the exigencies of the service. Such a development would be in line with the great expansion of further education planned for the nation as a whole, and we are confident that education authorities, co-operating regularly with chief constables in the ways we have envisaged, would show great interest and helpfulness in promoting the continued general education of young constables.

307. Two points should be added. First, our proposals for improving the educational assessment of applicants to the police service do not imply that we regard educational qualifications as more important than integrity and mental and physical fitness. As we said in our interim report, all these requirements are essential. Secondly, we would make it clear that in no circumstances do we contemplate the educationist's having more than an advisory function in the selection of police recruits. The responsibility is the chief constable's and it must remain unimpaired.

Recruitment of future senior officers

308. In our interim report we expressed our concern at the lack of well educated recruits to the police service. The facts may be summarised as follows. We have come across no recent instance of a university graduate entering the service; only about 1 per cent of recruits have two or more GCE passes at advanced level; a further 10 per cent have five or more GCE subjects at ordinary level; and in addition, some 20 per cent have one to four GCE subjects at ordinary level. These figures relate to recruits accepted in the usual way at 19 plus. Boys entering the service as cadets tend to possess rather higher educational qualifications. On the basis of these figures we commented that, while the police service attracts a substantial number of grammar school boys, most of them belong to the lower half of those who leave the grammar school at the age of 16.

309. In August, 1961, Your Majesty's Secretary of State presented to Parliament a White Paper[37] containing proposals to alter the training arrangements of the police in England and Wales, and these proposals have

implications for recruitment.

310. Under the Government's proposals a new course for constables, of twelve months' duration, is to be established at the Police College. Entrants will be selected from those who have obtained the highest marks in the examination in police subjects for promotion to sergeant; and an officer who successfully completes the course will receive automatic promotion to sergeant in his force. Similarly, it is proposed to reserve, for sergeants who qualify by examination, a promotion of the vacancies on the present six months' course which prepares sergeants for promotion to inspector. (At present all the sergeants admitted to this course are nominated by their police authority or chief officer of police.) A third proposal is to introduce a senior staff course, of a primarily professional character, designed to equip officers of the rank of inspector or above for the highest posts in the service. This course will be of six months' duration.

311. The Government's White Paper remarks that these new arrangements will make an important contribution to the development of the service; and, after recalling the well-established principle that senior officers should be drawn from the service itself, it proceeds

". . . It is therefore important, if the Service is to produce enough leaders of the right calibre, that training of the right sort should be made available to those who have demonstrated that they are suitable for higher rank. It is also important that the Service should be seen to offer attractive prospects for the recruit of good quality and that he should feel that he will be given the opportunity to use his talents to the best advantage. The working out of the new schemes outlined above will have to be carefully watched; but it is believed that they will improve the ability of the Police Service to attract and train its own leaders, and enable the Police College to make an even greater contribution than at present to the efficiency of the Service."

312. We are extremely concerned that the conditions of entry and promotion prospects of the police service should be such as will attract a sufficient number of recruits who are likely to make good chief constables and other senior officers twelve, fifteen or twenty years hence. In the past, many men with distinguished careers lacked a university education, but this situation is rapidly changing: young men of ability now tend in increasing numbers to proceed to the universities. Consequently a system of police recruiting which shows no evidence of success in attracting a sufficient proportion of entrants of graduate standard endangers the future leadership of the service. Improvements in pay and new training arrangements will not by themselves cure this defect. The police play a vital part in our national life and well-being and it is deplorable that they, to a far greater extent than any of the other public services, law, commerce, industry or indeed any major branch of our national life, should for years have been failing to recruit anything like their proper share of able and well educated young men. We do not suggest that graduates are necessarily more likely than others to make effective chief constables; Our concern is simply that the police today are not securing a sufficient share of the better educated section of the community.

313. The reason for this failure is not, in our view, that the police service is inherently unattractive as a career, nor is it primarily attributable to the absence of a sure and speedy way to the top. It lies in the neglect of those responsible to adjust the opening stages of a police career, in the way that

other professions have found it necessary to do, so as to attract able candidates. It cannot be doubted that it is the early prospects that influence most young people to choose one career rather than another. Nor does it call for any great insight or a deep knowledge of psychology to understand how the police service must appear at a disadvantage in this respect compared with almost any other profession today.

314. Our first recommendation concerns the minimum period of service before promotion to sergeant. At present a constable must, save in exceptional circumstances, serve three years after probation—a total of five years' service—before he can be promoted. The period of five years must normally include two years' "ordinary outside duty". We do not accept that initiation into the duties of a constable or preparation for the rank of sergeant need always take so long. No doubt in most cases the period is not inappropriate, but we see no sufficient reason why a chief constable should be fettered, to a degree unparalleled in any other occupation, in the exercise of his own judgment as to when a man is ready for greater responsibility. Moreover, from the point of view of a graduate considering the service as a career, a delay of five years, which cannot be altered to take account of his age, and gives him no chance to prove maturity and aptitude above the average, must appear an intolerable obstacle. We accordingly recommend that the minimum qualifying period for promotion to sergeant be reduced from five to three years, and that suitable modification be made in the length of service before a candidate may offer himself for the qualifying examination.

315. Our next proposal involves only a change of nomenclature, but one which some of us regard as not unimportant as a further means of improving the attractiveness of a police career. In our first report we stressed the unusual nature of the constable's responsibility compared with others of a subordinate rank. By the same token the police sergeant performs duties which are not to be compared with those of the army non-commissioned officer from whom his title is borrowed. We heard evidence to the effect that the title "sergeant" is an honoured and popular one within the police service. But his name and his badge of rank are against him in the eyes of a potential entrant, who may be misled into thinking that the equivalent of commissioned rank in the police is not attained until the third rung in the ladder. A number of us think that consideration should be given to changing the title of sergeant to some such title as sub-inspector, with an appropriate modification of the badge of rank.

316. None of these measures will have any success in bringing men of high calibre into the service if they are not joined with a resolve on the part of those responsible for recruiting to use every available means to attract this kind of entrant. It is in our opinion vital that the concept of the police service as a career in which men of the highest ability can find their proper place should be maintained. We do not doubt that Your Majesty's Ministers are aware of the urgency of this requirement, and they ought not to shrink from bold and even controversial measures in order to secure it. It is essential, too, that the police service as a whole should accept the need not only for improvement in the general quality of recruits but also for an increased intake of outstanding men.

37Cmnd. 1450

It is almost a certainty that for many years to come the

police of England and Wales will not require candidates for police constable to be college or university graduates. This prediction may be offered for many reasons, prime of which is the centralized nature (when viewed with police organization in the United States as a frame of reference) of the British police. This does not include a prediction that the British police will not heartily encourage men to seek university training, both prior to police service entry and following. Most certainly in England and Wales as in the United States such intellectual training and discipline is on the upswing.

When one assesses the meaning of Royal Commission Report paragraphs presented previously, he must be informed that in spite of many common factors and a similar heritage which, in many respects, linked citizens of the original thirteen United States to Great Britain, some striking differences in police organization emerged and mark contemporary police administration in the United States. He should be informed of the following:

1. The American police service is highly decentralized. There is no federal governmental control which insures standards, provides direction or incentive, prescribes organization, jurisdiction, financial support, or in any other fashion directly superimposes itself upon the administration of police at all levels of government.

2. American police officers, excepting those in the federal service, are not agents of the President of the United States or the national government. They are agents of the particular level of government they serve.

3. American local, county, and state police forces receive no federal financial support and are not inspected for compliance with arbitrary performance standards by agents of the federal service. Federal law enforcement bodies, of course, are supported by federal funds, but no agency or device exists to universally coordinate and appraise adequacy and effectiveness of federal law enforcement services. The principle of joint national-local responsibility, symbolized in Britain through the centralizing influence exercised by the Home Office, does not exist in the United States. And it is not likely to.

4. There is no federal machinery binding upon all levels of government which establishes uniformity of salaries, conditions of service and retirement programming for the nation's police personnel. Nor is there a national police federation or union which represents the rank and file in their quest for improving working conditions and police administration.

The student must understand that police organization in contemporary America is an expression of the democratic form of government found in the United States. Such a political philosophy provides for government organization at several levels with reluctance towards centralizing police power or authority at any one level. The result finds that no town, village or hamlet is too small to have its own police force and police organizations function at five district levels of government; federal, state, county, city and township. In addition, there are some areas which have formed special protection districts and have organized forces for law enforcement. Present police organization in the United States is a direct product of its historical antecedents, flavored by tradition and, from time to time, rendered more complex by the creation of special purpose forces as enforcement instrumentalities to combat unique problems. There are about 42,000 separate police forces in the United States.

This differs from police organization in England and Wales where only 125 county and city police forces and the London Metropolitan Police serve the country's approximately forty-seven million population which resides in 58,347 square miles (or an area about the size of California). There are about 82,000 police personnel in England and Wales, a police-to-population ratio of about 1.75 officers per 1,000 citizens. So in the United States about 330,000 agents of public justice in the nation's 42,000 police jurisdictions conform to no fixed or definable universal minimum standard for entry into police service and the departments have no single accepted organization structure, public responsibility or general efficiency level. Among these forces are some of the best law enforcement agencies that have been developed anywhere in the world, at any level of government. Others are in the process of changing over from antiquated methods and are now embracing new techniques for popular control, general supervision and improved day-to-day functioning. Included are a considerable number of agencies that have failed to show any sign of renaissance and seem bypassed by constructive impulses that have brought development and progress to the first two groups. These last police forces constitute a burden on the entire machinery of justice and are detrimental to the process of achieving a professional police service held in esteem by the citizens of the nation.

In conclusion, efforts which the British police are making to attract more promising officers is consistent with the will of Doctor Patrick Colquhoun as expressed in his 1796 *Treatise on the Police of the Metropolis:*

Next to the blessings which a Nation derives from an excellent Constitution and system of general laws are those advantages which result from a well regulated and energetic plan of Police conducted and enforced with Purity, Activity, Vigilance and Discretion.

The Police have a fair claim, while they act properly, to be esteemed as the civil defenders of the lives and properties of the people.

Anything which can heighten in any degree the respectibility of the office of Constable adds to the security of the State and to the safety of the life and property of the individual.

Chapter 7

LETTERS OF SUPPORT

The sheriff's letter requesting the higher minimum educational entry standard presented in Chapter 3 was supported by several personal letters. Writers who supported the concept ranged from a United States Supreme Court Justice to the academic community to informed persons in the public service in the greater Multnomah County area. The support expressed from such a variety of quarters was an impressive ground swell.

Several thoughts emerged as paramount: (1) the Civil Service Commission should take favorable action upon the sheriff's request; (2) it was proper as well as progressive that the sheriff should seek to elevate rather than lower standards; (3) the standard established by the Civil Service Commission is closely related to the level and effectiveness of police service in Multnomah County ten, twenty and thirty years hence on the premise that the men selected this year and next constitute the core group from which police leadership in years to come will be selected; (4) police work in the space age in becoming ever more complex; and (5) the policeman's task is ever more difficult in the face of constantly changing criminal laws of arrest, search, seizure, interrogation and an alarming pattern of persons flouting law and order by chiding and resisting police.

There was a feeling which seemed to pervade most letters which urged the Civil Service Commission to help the sheriff's office lead the field of law enforcement and achieve a breakthrough long overdue in law enforcement circles at state, county and local levels.

The text of many supporting letters follows.

Former United States Supreme Court Associate Justice, who presently is United States Ambassador to the United Nations, the Honorable Arthur J. Goldberg, asserted:

It is with interest that I have learned that the Multnomah County Sheriff's Office requires two years of college before one can take the civil service examination for deputy sheriff. I also am advised that it is hoped in the near future to raise this standard to a Bachelor's degree. I am one who shares your view that the demands made on police officers in a complex modern world warrant the highest educational standards. Law enforcement officers are a most important part of the administration of justice and high qualifications of character and educational background contribute materially to the effectiveness of their work.

The Honorable Arno H. Denecke, Associate Justice of the Oregon Supreme Court, wrote:

I definitely share your view that it is essential to raise the standards for law enforcement officers. Rightly or wrongly, the courts are requiring much more of police officers today than was required five or six years ago. In the constitutional fields of search and seizure, right to counsel, etc., a police officer must be able to absorb a quick re-education in techniques necessitated by the rapid changes in these areas.

Because of the constitutional limitations being placed on law enforcement, it seems imperative that police officers devise new techniques or more highly developed present techniques of crime detection.

The Honorable Tom McCall, Oregon Secretary of State, wrote with enthusiasm as he expressed his opinion:

This office has noted with interest your efforts to require a Bachelor's degree as a prerequisite to taking the Civil Service examination for deputy sheriff in Multnomah County.

As one who has lent editorial support to creation of the State Police Training Advisory Committee and to expansion of the law enforcement curriculum of some of our colleges, I heartily approve your advocacy of this higher standard. With society becoming increasingly complex, it is mandatory for all of us in positions of responsibility to espouse the goal of true professional status for police, and your program is an essential step in this direction.

Mr. Lee M. Bown, Executive Secretary of the Oregon State Advisory Board on Police Standards and Training, Salem, wrote:

I heartily approve your efforts to raise the educational require-
ments for applicants to your department. The profession of law
enforcement is now confronted with a challenge from our complex
society which demands a college level of education.

While other attributes are required of those entering the profes-
sion an applicant with advanced schooling can better assimulate
training to meet the demand of our laws, as interpreted by the
courts; better understand the problems of domestic disturbances,
mental, juvenile and racial problems to mention a few; which are
continually experienced.

These are my personal views and not necessarily those of the
Board Members and should be considered accordingly.

Oregon's Public Defender, Lawrence A. Aschenbrenner,
also favored the elevation of the educational standard:

. . . I am briefly setting forth my views as to what the educa-
tional qualifications of today's police officer should be.

It is now acknowledged generally that the problems of law enforce-
ment engendered by the recent United States Supreme Court deci-
sions of Escobedo vs. Illinois and Mapp vs. Ohio will never be
solved unless the caliber of law enforcement officers is elevated.

In earlier days, confessions secured from an accused were re-
sponsible for the vast majority of convictions. Likewise, illegally
seized evidence was admissible against an accused upon his
trial. Under the new law, confessions and admissions unless
secured pursuant to the high, rigid and somewhat technical re-
quirements of the United States Supreme Court are no longer ad-
missible against an accused. Also, illegally seized evidence can
no longer be introduced against an accused. To bring a criminal
to justice today has become an exceedingly difficult and sensitive
task requiring highly trained and educated personnel. No longer,
in my judgment, will a grade school or even a high school diploma
suffice. If society is to be protected, college educated police
officers must become the rule and not the rare exception.

The most encouraging news which has come to my attention
during the past year in the battle of law enforcement, was the
word that your Department has a minimum standard of two years
of college. But |encouraging as this progress has been, it still
does not go far enough.

Surely every police officer in whose hands society puts its very collective life should have a college degree. This is certainly no time to reduce your standards, but to raise them.

Mr. Duane C. Lemley, Consultant to the Oregon Council on Crime and Delinquency, Portland, supported the proposal that the educational standard be raised:

My view of law enforcement has been from the vantage point of my work and experience in court and institutional settings. Therefore, the scientific and technical aspects of crime investigation are not areas about which I am competent to comment.

However, one of the responsibilities of law enforcement which is extremely important from my point of view and which makes a great difference to the other parts of a corrections system is the impression created by law enforcement on the offender. It has been demonstrated that police who have a basic knowledge about human behavior can make their contact with the offender one of helping him face up to his responsibility as a citizen. Extremely punitive handling by police can create hostile attitudes in the offender which are extremely difficult to change.

Modern-day police need to know a great deal about the law and the rights of the offenders due in part to recent supreme court decisions. In addition law enforcement personnel continue to be the first judges. Decisions have to be made on the spot as to whether a warning will suffice or whether action of a court is needed. More and more police are becoming involved in family disputes which require tact, skill and judgment of a high order.

A final point is that police need to identify themselves as an important part of the correctional system. If law enforcement personnel are to be effective they must know something about law and about the responsibilities and limitations of the courts, of correctional institutions and of community agencies such as clinics for alcoholic offenders, family counseling agencies, public welfare programs, etc.

This brief and incomplete description of skills and knowledge which from my point of view are needed by police today require that candidates be selected who possess solid educational backgrounds at the college level. A basic knowledge of law, human behavior, the courts, state and local correctional programs and community agencies can best be taught in regular college programs.

These, of course, must be supplemented by special college or inservice training courses in police science and other areas peculiar to the requirements of good law enforcement.

The Oregon State Sheriff's Association supported Sheriff Clark's proposal when Secretary-Treasurer W. L. "Bud" Mekkers wrote on behalf of the Association:

On behalf of the Association's membership, and in light of a resolution passed at our summer meeting, we heartily endorse your efforts to secure higher educational requirements for deputy sheriffs.

Recognizing the growing complexity of the law enforcement mission and the heightened demands on police officers everywhere, we are much aware of the increasingly important role that education will play in the recruitment of personnel.

We further recognize that the universal acceptance of the police officer as a professional man depends in large measure on the individual's level of formal education and specialized training. Each local elevation of recruitment standards aids the efforts of each of us to upgrade our own departments and hastens the day when every officer must be accorded the degree of respect that his job and his training deserve.

Multnomah County Police Union Local 117, affiliated with the American Federation of State, County and Municipal Employees, wrote supporting the proposal. President Allen A. McDaniels said succinctly:

We are in full accord with your efforts to upgrade our police officers.

Multnomah County District Attorney George Van Hoomissen supported the request to raise the standards when he wrote:

I understand that the Multnomah County Civil Service Commission will soon undertake a reevaluation of some of the requirements for eligibility to take the civil service examination for Multnomah County deputy sheriff.

It is my understanding that the educational requirements for eligibility to take this examination will come under particular scrutiny by the Multnomah County Civil Service Commission. I wish to state categorically my opinion that a minimum of two years of college-level education should now be considered an absolute prerequisite to eligibility for appointment as a Multnomah County deputy sheriff. I make this recommendation based upon my personal, daily observation of the functions, duties and responsibilities of law enforcement officers in our county.

It is my understanding that at the present time Multnomah County requires deputy sheriff applicants to show an educational equivalent of two years of college work. It would be inconceivable and a great disservice to this community if this requirement, now in effect, were to be reduced or relaxed. The duties and responsibilities of law enforcement officers are becoming increasingly more complex. It is no longer sufficient or adequate that a peace officer be physically competent to cope with increasingly technical problems. Today's police officer must possess the mental ability and educational background which can only come from formal training in the post-high school educational process. He must understand psychology, logic, English, speech, sociology, philosophy and law. He must be able to comprehend and apply the complex laws within the jurisdiction of the sheriff. He must be able to adapt instantly to changing court decisions and to communicate both orally and in writing with his superiors, prosecuting attorneys, jurors and judges.

Rather than considering reducing the educational requirements for deputy sheriff, we should be seriously considering raising those requirements at the earliest practical time to three years of college-level work and, in the not too distant future, to a bachelor's degree from an accredited college or university.

I cannot overemphasize my personal belief, based on the most intimate experience with the problems of law enforcement, that it would be a tragedy of major proportions should the Multnomah County Civil Service Commission reduce the educational requirements now established for eligibility to take the examination for Multnomah County deputy sheriff. No useful purpose could possibly be served by reducing those educational requirements at this time. I feel confident in believing that every professional in law enforcement would strongly recommend against the reduction of the educational requirements for eligibility to take this examination.

I would strongly urge the Multnomah County Civil Service Commission to raise the minimum educational requirement for eligibility

for Multnomah County deputy sheriff to three years of college-
level work by 1968 and a bachelor's degree by 1970.

The clergy supported the Sheriff's proposal. Doctor Richard
M. Steiner, Minister of the First Unitarian Church, Portland,
wrote:

I am at the moment serving on a (Portland) City Club committee
involving policies of law enforcement on the city level, and I am
increasingly impressed with the necessity of having our law
enforcement officers better trained and with a higher educational
level of attainment. We are living in a very complex society, and
with the courts demanding stricter rules of obtaining evidence it
is obvious that a higher degree of intelligence and of knowledge
is required of those charged with law enforcement.

I wish to commend you for your efforts in seeking higher standards
for your deputies.

Oregon Regional Director Paul B. Bender of the National
Conference of Christians and Jews, Inc., supported Sheriff
Clark's position:

As you know, Police Community Relations is one of the major
program areas of N.C.C.J. beginning with our pioneer efforts nine
years ago in establishing a National Institute at Michigan State
University. Our regional seminars, in addition to the continuing
national one, have revealed the great need for upgrading the
standards of law enforcement qualifications to keep pace with
the great social changes that our country is experiencing.

Your present requirement of two years of college has been a sig-
nificant step forward, one in which the community will take pride.
It is our hope, however, that this can soon be raised to a Bache-
lor's Degree. This would be in keeping with the consensus of
opinion and need expressed nationally and certainly be a major
move in achieving the professional status we covet for all law
enforcement personnel.

The academic community was on record as favoring the increase in minimum educational standard for deputy sheriff positions. Doctor Charles R. Adrian, Chairman of the Department of
Political Science, Michigan State University, East Lansing,
Michigan, and former Director of the Institute for Community

Development and Services at Michigan State University wrote:

> . . . You are showing real leadership in the development of professional police departments in metropolitan counties.

> I was especially impressed by your requirement of at least two years of college. It seems to me that this is one of the best approaches to the professionalization of police work and one of the best ways to increase the status of police officers anywhere. Admission and successful completion of at least part of a college career is in itself an indication of intelligence. In addition, spendint time in college is helpful in producing maturity and sophistication, both of which are needed in law enforcement. It is true that much of the routine work by a policeman or deputy sheriff could be handled by a happy moron but this is not the case with the critical decisions that are so important in the shaping of the image of a department of law enforcement officers generally. (Intelligence, maturity, and sophistication can all, of course, be found in the person who has never attended college, but the statistical probabilities of finding such persons are vastly greater among those with a college education.)

> . . . Competition for persons with the degree is considerable and you might not yet be able to compete effectively at that level, but I would urge you to move in that direction as quickly as you can. I feel strongly that this is one of the ways in which police and sheriff departments can improve the public image of the law enforcement officer.

Doctor S. Sidney Ulmer, chairman of the Department of Political Science at the University of Kentucky wrote a strong supporting statement and cited his own scholarly interest in supreme court matters as a primary basis for his conclusion that the move upwards in minimum educational standard is fully warranted:

> It is good to see that Sheriff Don Clark is making a real effort to raise the professional standards of his force. Although it will obviously take several years for the advantages of this policy to be fully realized, it is a safe bet that the County, and the City of Portland, will benefit from this policy in the long run.

> The decision to raise professional standards and qualifications of police officers is certainly quite in keeping with the new, and

much more important role that law enforcement officers are called upon to play in our society. As the metropolitan areas of the nation continue to expand, police officers must perform new tasks and play new roles. In some places, the answer is found by increasing the size of police forces. I note that the President has recently asked Congress to appropriate an additional $1,879,000 for police services in the nation's capital, while in New York, the Mayor was recently forced to ask the City Council for an additional 6 million to pay for expanded services. But these are the exceptions: in most metropolitan areas, the increase in urban population means a decrease in the ratio of police officers per thousand of population. It is this fact, more than any other, that makes it imperative that the calibre of entering personnel be constantly improved.

My own interest in the Supreme Court leads me to conclude that there is another reason why police forces across the nation must try to raise the professional standards and qualifications of their new recruits. As you know, the Supreme Court has handed down an important series of decisions dealing with the rights of those who are accused of crime. The former Commissioner of Police in New York City, Michael Murphy recently suggested that these decisions have "unduly hampered" law enforcement agencies. Although he may have dramatized the point, it is certainly true that the decisions of the Court on confessions and searches and seizures have put a heavier burden on the police. Convictions in the future will have to rely more on what Justice Arthur Goldberg called "extrinsic evidence independently secured through skillful investigation." It is my opinion that this task can only be performed adequately by mature, educated, career-oriented law enforcement officers.

By raising standards in the largest metropolitan area in the state, the Sheriff is setting a good example for smaller counties to follow. His efforts to break with the past will undoubtedly be resisted by those who still believe that all one has to do to get a police officer, is to stick a badge on a man's coat. But in the long run, even they will be convinced that the policy is sound and progressive.

In closing let me request that you keep in touch with us. Members of this department are occasionally asked to consult with local officials. Your experiences in upgrading recruitment standards may be of some use to us in performing this advisory function.

Colonel David A . McCandless, Director of the Southern Police Institute, University of Louisville, Kentucky, wrote a forceful letter supporting the sheriff's request:

You deserve great credit for your efforts in behalf of profession- alization of law enforcement forces. You have indeed pioneered in your efforts to improve minimum entry educational standards and in obtaining the highest type of selection procedures. It takes great strength of character to be a leader instead of temporizing and waiting for others to furnish vital leadership.

The requirement, by the Multnomah County Sheriff's Office, of two-year College or University training for applicants is a great stride forward in my opinion. I hope very much that this require- ment will not be rescinded except under emergency circum- stances. This trend, toward College or University pre-entry train- ing, is clearly discernable and is, I think, an excellent one. I suspect that in the not too distant future, the more progressive law enforcement departments will require the Bachelor's degree.

You will recall that V. A. Leonard in POLICE ORGANIZATION AND MANAGEMENT said, "Experience has shown that even four years of specific preparation at the University level, with the total resources of a major educational institution geared to the task, represent too short a time in which to prepare a man for entry into police service." As the work of our law enforcement officers becomes daily more complex, certainly ever greater educational attainments will be required.

The Honorable Quinn Tamm, Executive Director of the In- ternational Association of Chiefs of Police, Inc., wrote to lend his support and the backing of his organization to the improve- ment of educational standards:

The role of the pace setter, in our business as in most others, is never an easy one. Unfortunately, however, we have found that in five years of conducting management surveys of inefficient police departments, one of the common fundamental deficiencies has been the inadequate education and training of personnel.

As you know, we have just devoted the May (1965) issue of THE POLICE CHIEF magazine to the topic of police education. We are firmly committed to a program that will establish entrance requirements for police personnel at such a level as to make professional service a realistic goal. At the first meeting of our Advisory Councils on Police Education and Police Training held in February of this year at Williamsburg, Virginia, the group adopted the position that the educational requirements for police service should be established at the highest possible level consistent with the availability of qualified people. This means simply that if a department is able to hire all men with bachelor degrees because of the fact that they have a college or university program from which to draw, then that should be their minimum requirement. On the other hand, agencies that are unable to competently staff themselves with fully qualified persons may have to settle temporarily for those who bring only two years of educational experience to the job. Only in those cases where the labor market cannot provide professionally educated people should an agency seek or accept individuals without college backgrounds. In these deliberations, we also adjusted our thinking in terms of high school degrees or the GED certificate to the point where we feel that the educational requirement should be stated not in those terms but rather in terms of persons whose work in high school reflects the ability of the individual to go on to programs of higher learning. As you can see, we are contemplating an educational standard that would be based upon a candidate's successful completion of the College Entrance Examination Board or some similar evaluative test.

As you well know, the most fundamental factor in determining the service capability of a law enforcement agency is the ability of the people who staff that agency. To reduce your educational requirement where there is no apparent difficulty in the recruitment of an adequate number of qualified persons would represent a gross disservice to the citizens within your jurisdiction. Furthermore, it would indicate that those who did take such a backward step neither understand nor appreciate the importance or the complexity of law enforcement in a democratic society.

Our concern with the professionalization of law enforcement is based upon our desire to see the citizens of this country receiving the finest level of police service. If there attaches to the individual officer any additional stature or recognition by virtue of the fact that law enforcement is in fact a profession, this is an ancillary benefit.

Doctor George D. Eastman, former Chief of Police in Seattle, Washington, and Pontiac, Michigan, and former Superintendent

of the Port Authority of New York and presently on the staff of
Public Administration Service, Chicago, Illinois, presented a
provocative letter which spoke of the complexities of contemporary police service:

*The complexities of contemporary law enforcement extend the
full range from the simple provision of geographical information
to a tourist to the investigation of organized crime and espionage.
To cope with such a broad scope of responsibilities, today's law
enforcement agency must seek the most qualified personnel available.*

*While the past two decades have brought forth many significant
changes in the nature of the crime and traffic problems, primary
improvement in police service has been largely in the material
and equipment made available for law enforcement. Scientific
techniques researched and developed in other fields have been
adopted and adapted by progressive police and sheriff's departments. Unfortunately, while the quality of equipment and services
available to law enforcement has risen, development and adoption
of standards for selection and promotion of police personnel have
not been given the same detailed and thoughtful attention.*

*We have today, therefore, a situation wherein a modern, mobile,
generally well educated society is insisting on a quantity and
quality of service not previously necessary; yet, in many instances,
relatively untrained and/or uneducated personnel must attempt to
meet demands for service with insufficient professional or technical competency.*

*The capability of most police agencies to successfully educate
as well as train entrants is severely limited by restrictions of
time, budget, and manpower. It may be anticipated that, with
growing needs for service by other departments and agencies
paralleling the increased requirements of the police department,
particular attention to police education and training needs and
costs could not be given at the expense or to the neglect of other
important services. To offset this, among other reasons, law
enforcement agencies must necessarily upgrade entrance requirements, taking full advantage of the rapidly expanding pool of
college students and graduates now available for employment.*

*The experience of many of those agencies which require or en-
courage college level education for police officers indicates that*

those officers not only perform well as patrolmen, but are especially valuable to the community when they begin to advance to positions of responsibility through the promotional process. In effect, these departments have taken a page from the guidebooks of business, industry and the federal government, where a college education is fast becoming a condition of employment in many positions of present or potential responsibility.

With the educational advantages of the Multnomah County area, it seems especially important to seriously consider retention of your present two-year college requirement. When, practically, your recruiting base is adequate, consideration may be given to stiffening your requirement to four years or its equivalent. Standards should be raised, in all respects, to the maximum compatible with department needs.

E. F. Holladay, Chief of the fifty-five man Monterey Park, California, Police Department supported the position paper:

For years administrators in law enforcement have known that the shortest route to professional status was to elevate standards and train personnel. However, unlike the policeman twenty years ago whose responsibilities and authority were comparatively stable, the modern officer must continually train and inform himself if he is to operate successfully in the light of increasing limitations on his actions by court decisions.

More important, current civil strife spreading hate, pitting neighbor against neighbor in ideological if not physical combat, places even the most remote community under threat of mob and riot conditions wherein only calm and courageous men of high personal ethics and abilities of self restraint would be able to restore law and order.

We do not argue that academic background will provide these qualities; however, in modern society the young man who is not pursuing higher education presents a question as to his interest in self-betterment. Therefore, he may be less than complimentary to a progressive organization. Further, his apparent lack of interest in education is an indicated resistance to training and/or change.

Approximately twenty-five years ago law enforcement began requiring a high school diploma or GED equivalent as a prerequisite to appointment. Monterey Park was one of the first cities to make the requirement in 1936. Presently, the City of Walnut Creek requires its police officer candidates to have graduated from college. Elsewhere in the state Berkeley, San Jose, Sunnyvale, El Monte and Costa Mesa require two years of college.[1]

It is generally agreed that the time is overdue for upgrading the requirements as these cities have done. Usually the first consideration is the shortage of manpower with present standards and the fear that further restriction would endanger the recruiting program. However, in personal contacts with the chiefs of El Monte and Costa Mesa, I learned that the college requirements seemed to attract an even greater number of applicants who were able to qualify at all levels of the selection process.

Chief Robert Bockhacker of the 60-man Vernon, California, Police Department reported on that city's recent increase in standards:

The City of Vernon, California, is an industrial city of approximately five square miles. The resident population consists of about two hundred and the daily working population consists of about sixty-five thousand.

The Police Department has sixty-two sworn personnel; it is not Civil Service, and the Chief of Police has been authorized by the City Council to appoint police officers and to use whatever testing media he deems proper. I have been Chief of this department for the past twelve years, and during this period, have increased the educational requirements for applicants from graduation from high school to the present thirty Units of college. There is no

[1]Chief Holladay's comment about standards in the 1930's makes timely the following 1926 assertion by Lent D. Upson of the Detroit Bureau of Governmental Research. It provides ample contrast to disclose that in almost forty years the American police service has significantly improved its quality of personnel:

> In most large cities patrolmen are selected on the merit system but usually they have only a common school education and are recruited for the most part from the ranks of labor, largely from unskilled trades. The qualifications are standard throughout the country—good physical condition, minimum height of five feet eight and one-half or nine inches, ability to read and write, United States citizenship, residence in the city, and good character. The entrance examination consists of a medical examination and a written test designed to show the applicant's knowledge of the city and his ability to read and write. In addition, an investigation of his character is made. The Detroit police department, which is not under the jurisdiction of the civil service board, once experimented for a short time with psychiatric examinations, every applicant being given a standard intelligence test and an examination by a psychiatrist.

Lent D. Upson, *Practice of Municipal Administration.* New York, The Century Co., 1926, p. 330. SGC & DEC.

doubt in my mind that the educational requirements will be raised as time goes by; and the only thing that precludes my requiring higher education at the present time, is the inadequate number of applicants.

I feel that increased educational requirements are obvious. The Supreme Court's decisions, for instance, must not only be followed, but above all, they must be understood. The more education the officer has, the more he is prepared to understand the complex decisions handed down by the Courts.

It has been my obsersation that most people have the highest regard for the Federal Bureau of Investigation and, as you know, the educational requirements for agents exceed those of any sheriffs or police department.

William H. Berlin, Jr., Chief of the Hermosa Beach, California, Police Department urged that law enforcement agencies increase standards:

Our department has the minimum requirement of sixty units, and we are presently considering requesting that this minimum be increased to a Bachelors degree. We find that there are many desirable candidates available for openings within our department, with their Bachelors/degree, thus when we can obtain higher educated individuals for this complex task of law enforcement, we select them; the reasons are many, here are but a few examples:

Candidates with the minimum of two years of college are easier to train on the complexities of changes in the rules of evidence, search and seizure, arrest and court technique. They are more susceptible to training on specialty items, such as internal and external intelligence, public relations, budgeting and auxiliary services, they are more adept at adjusting to situations that require clear thinking and precise action.

I strongly would urge you and other law enforcement personnel to seek higher educational standards from your Civil Service Commission, and resist any program that would downgrade law enforcement. We cannot afford to reduce standards in any manner, shape or form, and we cannot afford the luxury of having uneducated persons representing law and order.

Chief Strevell G. Taylor of San Buenaventura, California,

reported that since 1951 his department has required all personnel, either before or after appointment, to complete at least two years of college education. Drawing upon his thirty-seven years of police service, Chief Taylor urged that standards be elevated when conditions permit:

> I have found after thirty-seven years of police experience that if we intend to be recognized professionally we must meet academic standards comparable to those of other professions. We must meet those standards to fulfill the expectation and demands of John Doe Citizen of his servants, Police Officers.

> Mr. Citizen entrusts to his officers the care and welfare of his family along with the safe keeping of his worldly goods. He expects and demands intelligent individuals capable of meeting his every demand for law enforcement. Intelligence to cope with the intelligent criminal, to meet with and be accepted in all walks of life.

> The professional standards give ground for higher salaries commensurante to the capability, trust, responsibility, and reliability, demanded of the enforcement officer.

> The higher standard of qualifications or office material should and will enlist the service of those individuals who will be dedicated to law enforcement and not the average person taking a job because he can find none better or some person looking for security rather than productivity.

> Since 1951, this department has required all persons, either befor or after appointment, to attain at least two years of College Police Science and it was my intention to recruit future officer material from those who have made their scholastic preparedness for the position and responsibility attached there-to, and as further qualification, all applicants must pass the Army GET test with not less than 125 IQ (original scale 97-118).

> Personally, I can see no reason why anyone would consider lowering the qualifications of a Police Officer, especially where there are so many Police Science majors to be had if the salary is inducive to the demand.

El Monte, California Police Chief Orval Davis reported on the El Monte experience with college-trained personnel. He also counted the advantages inherent in employing such persons.

Chief Davis's department includes over sixty sworn members:

> In considering our present standards we recognized the fact that
> police officers must deal with the broad field of human relations,
> human rights, protection of life and the protection of property
> under the most adverse of conditions. Within a very short span of
> time numerous changes in the law and the interpretation of the
> law takes place. Decisions concluded in the field by the officer
> are made under the worst possible conditions, and it has been
> estimated by educators in the criminal law field that in order to
> make the RIGHT legal decisions in this difficult setting today
> the police officer needs at least four times the amount of crimi-
> nal-legal knowledge required of the average law school graduate.
> To make a WRONG decision not only brings about problems for
> the police officer and his superiors, but for his legal entity as
> well. More and more the courts are finding the legal entity liable
> for the actions of their police officers and giving large financial
> settlements to the individual.

> Taking the above into consideration, this Department, in May,
> 1959, began requiring one year of college work at the entrance
> level, and increased this requirement in two years in November
> of 1963. During this period we have had no problems in recruit-
> ing well qualified personnel of the highest caliber. In fact, it has
> been our experience that our college requirement has aided us in
> competing with the metropolitan departments of this area such as
> the Los Angeles Police Department and the Los Angeles County
> Sheriff's Department for manpower. Since both of these Depart-
> ments pay over $50 per month more than we do we decided to
> seek why applicants who were on our list and at the same time on
> one or both of the above Departments' lists chose to accept em-
> ployment with us. Almost to a man they stated the reason they
> chose El Monte was that they felt a Department that required
> college work presented a more professional type police organiza-
> tion and afforded them the opportunity in the long run to be recog-
> nized for their individual efforts.

> Other advantages of employing college-trained men are many,
> ability to reason, ability to adjust, and ability to meet and handle
> the public to name but a few. We found, however, that one of the
> greatest single advantages gained is in the college-trained man's
> superior ability to write a report that is clear, concise, complete
> and comprehendable.

> I would like to take this opportunity to congratulate you and the

officials of your county who are responsible for leading the way
to what I believe is a better law enforcement program in Oregon.
As one who was somewhat of a pioneer in the field of college
work for law enforcement officers in my own area, I know per-
sonally of the many problems you are facing. I know that it is
small comfort, but it is always more difficult to be a leader than
a follower.

In closing, I would like to say that we feel our present standards
are necessary and essential to the duties, functions, and responsibilities of police work today and cannot be lowered without seriously affecting the quality and quantity of the performance of the members of this Department. It is our opinion that
the efficiency of today's law enforcement officer will have to
increase tremendously if we are to efficiently handle the ever
increasing burden of today's police problems. We feel that law
enforcement standards should be continually increased and we
are seriously looking forward to requiring a Bachelors degree at
the entrance level as soon as we feel sufficient manpower in this
category is available.

R. E. Roth, Chief in Costa Mesa, California, reported that
his city presently requires two years of college and that in the
near future his force may require a four-year degree as a minimum entry standard:

While an educational requirement of sixty units of college level
study is not the complete answer to professionalization, it does
go a long way toward that goal. We have found that officers recruited under this plan are easier to train, have generally better
ability to reason through a problem to a successful solution, and
are less inclined to lose sight of the responsibility they bear by
the nature of our work.

During the past twelve months since our requirements have become known we have added twelve additional men to our force.
All men meet this requirement and we are very pleased with their
performance. We recently were praised by our City Council for
our efficiency and good attitude.

Our complement is now full and we have men on the eligibility
list so we can say that we are able to fill our vacancies with
well-qualified men when they are needed.

We are very pleased with this phase of our selection process and *feel that in the very near future we may require a four-year degree as a few other California agencies now do.*

We feel law enforcement is becoming so complicated and difficult due to court decisions and the general attitude of the public that we must improve the ability of our personnel to be able to handle effectively the complex situations they will face more frequently in the future.

Chief Earl Reinbold of the 140-man Santa Monica, California Police Department spoke of that city's reason for elevating its educational standard:

The Santa Monica Police Department established the requirement of sixty credit hours of college for entrance officers in July, 1964, and in addition to this requirement the pay plan was modified wherein the applicant with two years of college starts at the second step. We have had fewer applicants take the examination but the persons who have passed the test have been of better caliber. The on-the-job excellence of applicants with two years of college has been gratifying to us.

We have sent approximately sixteen officers to the Los Angeles Police Academy Recruit Training School and only one officer has failed during the training. The norm for failure of officers at the academy is approximately 20 per cent. Our recruits are generally in the upper 50 per cent of the class. The college men are more amenable to training and seem to adapt to the rigors of modern day police work more easily than the High School graduate.

Throughout the Los Angeles area approximately 75 per cent of law enforcement personnel are attending some type of college and we find that our two year college men continue their schooling and eventually have four years of college.

The reason we started this program was that in checking our applicants we found the applicants who had college fared better on the examination and our background investigations were not revealing as many disqualifying conditions. If law enforcement is to complete with other professions in obtaining the most qualified personnel it is necessary that the standards be raised at the entrance level until we require a B.A. Degree. The complexity of modern day law enforcement makes it mandatory that our officers who entered the department with only a high school diploma attend college during their off time and this is very demanding on the officers and their families. The requirement prior to entrance will eliminate this pressure and allow the personnel to devote their full time to improvement in their law enforcement job.

One of the most meaningful letters addressed to the question before the Civil Service Commission came from Gene S. Muehleisen, Executive Officer of the California State Commission on Peace Officer Standards and Training, Sacramento, California. Muehleisen spoke at length about professionalizing the police service and recited several instances where departments have moved ahead in recent years. He concluded by asserting that it would be sound policy to hire four-year college men whenever the supply can meet the demand:

Confirming our recent conversations in Kentucky and Ohio concerning the serious problem of crime facing this Nation, we were pleased that President Lynden B. Johnson emphasized this point in his March 8 address to the Congress.

Among other things, the President stated that crime has become a malignant enemy in America's midst; that in dollars the cost of crime runs into tens of billions annually and the human costs are not measurable. He also stated that the problems run deep and will not yield to quick and easy answers; that crime will not wait while we pull it up by the roots.

The President also remarked that we must give new priority to methods and institutions of law enforcement.

In a message to all law enforcement officials, Director J. Edgar Hoover declared that "inadequate emphasis on the professionalization of law enforcement is one of our Nation's critical shortcomings in the fight against crime." He further stated that "it is vital then that law enforcement, colleges and universities, business and professional leaders, and local governments join forces to field a professional striking force in the unconditioned war against crime. More universities and colleges should be initiating and increasing courses of study oriented toward the development of a career police profession. Law enforcement must raise its sights, broaden its outlook, and insist on a higher caliber of performance."

Mr. Hoover also stated that "if our objective is to be reached, business, professional, and industrial leaders must crusade to overcome public apathy which breeds inadequacy and mediocrity. Their active support and influence are necessary for removal of the obstacles to the professionalization of law enforcement."

The complexities of the crime problem and of our changing society require a highly-trained and highly-educated police officer. One of the most overwhelming arguments favoring college education is presently occurring throughout the State of California. Over 11,000 full salaried in-service police officers are presently attending college on their own time and for the most part on their own money, because they have recognized the inadequacy of their training and education to cope with the great problems facing them on the streets of our cities and towns.

During the past few years, five California cities have increased their minimum educational requirement to two years of college, and seventeen additional cities have increased their requirements from between one and two years of college.

A recent recruit class of the Oakland Police Department numbering twenty men had a total of fourteen baccalaureate degrees. Chief Edward Toothman of that department has advised us that the speed with which the college-trained men reached a high level of performance is extremely encouraging and he intends to continue to recruit college men. Oakland employs approximately 650 sworn personnel.

The City of San Jose with a population of approximately 350,000 with 325 sworn personnel, has required two years of college as a recruitment standard since 1957. I recently discussed the high school vs. college graduate with San Jose police officials and they stated they would not revert to the high school level. Chief Blackmore states that a high factor in the low crime rate of San Jose is the fact that the college-trained officers are attacking the crime problem with great efficiency and at the same time enjoy prestige and high morale because they are respected for their college achievements.

The City of Berkeley retained two years of college as a minimum entrance requirement when they determined that police failures most frequently came from the men with the least amount of education.

The City of El Monte, California, has a department of approximately fifty-five sworn personnel. They currently require two years of college. When the last examination was conducted under the high school requirement, 107 candidates applied. The next examination under the two year college requirement produced ninety-five candidates. The Chief advised us that the caliber of the ninety-five candidates was extremely higher than the previous high school group. He further stated that he was greatly surprised at the high number of applicants and while interviewing the candidates, learned that they had applied because of the prestige in working for a department which requires college level recruits.

It is believed that a sound policy would be to hire four-year college men whenever the supply can meet the demands. This would be reduced to two years of college if the supply for four-year men was inadequate and reduced to high school graduation only in desperation when supplies of college men were entirely inadequate.

Our Commission takes this opportunity to commend the citizens of Multnomah County for being the first in the nation to require college-trained officers in their sheriff's department.

Chapter 8

CONCLUSION

The history of public education in the United States graphically illustrates the steady rise in the educational level of the population. During the 1920's and early depression years the term, "dropout" applied to persons who had not completed the eighth school grade. Thirty years later the dropout was one who had not completed the twelfth grade. Current trends point to a time in the future near when the term "dropout" may identify one who has not progressed beyond two years of post secondary schooling at a college, university, community college or equivalent educational institution. The proliferation of junior and community colleges testifies to the likelihood of further educational advances in terms of a higher general level of formal schooling.

Education, then, has neither been static nor is there reason to believe that the millenium has been reached. The transition from adolescence to a productive adult role in society bears little resemblance to the "automatic" transition made in primitive societies. No longer do tribal rites at age twelve qualify one for a place in adult society. Today's analogy to yesterday's tribal rite is the educational process, and this process continues to require an investment of more time as the general level of formal education rises. It does not take a student of social change to realize that the general level of educational achievement is relative to the times and that what constituted an adequate education yesterday or today may not constitute an adequate education tomorrow. Like the cost of living, the standard creeps constantly upward. An educational recession, furthermore, is not a likely prospect. If anything, the general level of education among Americans can be expected to accelerate as the pace of technological progress accelerates.

The concurrent effect of these trends, past and future, on minimum educational standards for law enforcement personnel should be obvious to every observer. The fact that law enforcement has not in the main kept pace with the growth that has occurred within other professions and callings makes the situation all the more critical. The law enforcement career field has certainly reached a sufficient degree of complexity and sophistication to justify college or university training. Few can say with conviction that law enforcement is holding its own, let alone gaining on, the general crime and public safety situation. The United States Department of Justice publication, *Uniform Crime Reports*, each year confirms this position.

The basic question in considering the merits of a college education for law enforcement personnel lies in assessing what will be gained by the individual officer. Much of the foregoing commentary has dealt with this question. Suffice it to say, at this point, that the process of education can be seen as one of developing an individual's inherent intellectual powers and skills to the fullest. It is apparent that developing an officer's power of perception, understanding and judgment will better enable him to deal with problems and situations more objectively, tolerantly and wisely. What more can the police administrator hope to achieve? What more can the citizen expect?

Beyond disciplining the mind, the advanced educational institutions also instill within the man a sense of dignity, both personal and as it applies to the worth and importance of law enforcement. The relationship and impact of the social sciences on law enforcement concerns also becomes more fully apparent, hence of practical value. It is further reasonable to posit that a sense of dedication to the concept of public service will be nurtured in the process. A man's desire to follow a public service career, coupled with education and his entry into police service, should lead to the ultimate professionalization of law enforcement. Law enforcement will not be granted professional status until the public recognizes it as warranting such standing and is willing to accept the field as one with a high degree of sophistication and a body of knowledge.

Law enforcement faces a dilemma as it strives for recognition. The importance of the police function must be recognized by the adult population of the United States. Yet the maturing

American child-student learns so little about it that is not distorted during the first twelve school years. The most readily available primer is the newspaper, the grade B movie, television and pulp magazines. Curbstone banter is another source of "information" where fact is overwhelmed by folklore and false conceptions. Yet law enforcement, because of the nature of the mission, its responsibilities to the public and its innate role of service must attain professional status if it is to stand on a par with law, theology, medicine and teaching. The public's respect for law enforcement will increase in direct proportion to the benefits which Mr. and Mrs. Citizen receive in the form of improved services and the story of law enforcement as it is understood by succeeding generations.

Crime and the public order are not the sole responsibilities of the police. The law enforcement function is but one of many cogs in the public service machinery that has evolved to administer justice and insure social order. The policies, programs, work and decisions of the courts, correctional institutions, parole and probation systems, juvenile authorities and every other public agency that encounters some aspect of the problem all share these responsibilities. So too do the churches, schools, philanthropic and private service organizations who are interested partners in the health and direction of our society.

The multiple causes of crime and social dislocation cannot be alleviated by the police alone regardless of their number, quality and financial resources. Poverty, alcoholism, narcotics addiction, racial and class tensions, economic deprivation, family disintegration and urbanization all contribute to the problem. These social ills ultimately concern every member of society and require an effort at every level and from every individual that is equal to the magnitude of the problem.

The effectiveness of the public mission, then, depends upon support from every segment of society, be it public and private agencies and organizations or the man on the street. Clearly, the social atmosphere within which the police must work has a direct bearing on the caliber of law enforcement that will be provided. This necessary support for good law enforcement must take the form of budgetary backing from the governmental hierarchy, but this backing, in turn, depends heavily upon the prevailing public attitude toward the police. A community whose members take law enforcement for granted or who are indifferent and even hostile to the police and what they seek to accomplish cannot expect to receive a high caliber of police service. This fact, however, does not allow the police administrator to unload his responsibility upon politicians or a lethargic public. Who is to be the prime mover in the crusade for professional police service administered by professionally prepared officers? Obviously this responsibility rests with the police administrator whose position and knowledge of needs and problems demands that he take the lead in dramatizing the facts of the law enforcement situation. Pressure can and should be brought to bear in a forceful but constructive manner.

Mobilizing public sentiment and drawing upon the support and resources of other public agencies and private organizations is a necessary and vital step in the process of upgrading law enforcement standards and attracting highly qualified men to the police ranks. The police stand at the focal point as justice is administered in the United States. Consequently, it is of paramount importance that the public attitude toward law enforcement and the administration of justice be shaped in a positive fashion. The relationship between education, police officers, crime suppression, public order, professional ethics, performance standards, over-all police efficiency and public respect for its police becomes obvious.

Respect is a tangible quality in that the degree to which it is present or absent is measurable, however imprecisely. It is also susceptible to violent aberrations, especially on the downward side, when individual police acts and departmental activities meet with widespread criticism. It does law enforcement and the concept of justice little good when citizens purport to respect the law in the abstract while their attitudes and actions indicate a basic disrespect for the police officer. The two are incompatible. It should be further recognized that the police alone can reconcile the contradiction by daily earning and maintaining respect over the long haul. This basic task falls to every police officer whose every action in every situation is subject to the scrutiny of so many. The scrutiny is inescapable just as is the conclusion that law enforcement personnel must be initially better equipped for the job.

Which comes first; the support and respect of the public or enlightened police policies, practices and personnel? One cannot wait upon the other. Both must be built concurrently and much of the job reverts to the police who must enunciate and drive home the urgency of the needs and problems and the importance of the objectives. The critical factor of human resources, upon which all else depends, is one that demands a high place on the priority list of police needs. The role of formal education in molding men for the police service is a subject that cannot be ignored or side-stepped by attacking the proposition that raised educational standards are valid for law enforcement personnel.

In addition to high preservice entry educational standards, the police need laws and ordinances which will aid them and other duly constituted authorities in coping with the nation's every increasing crime and traffic problems. Adequate numbers of personnel, adequate facilities and fiscal support sufficient to allow stepped-up training programs and increases in manpower are also vital to law enforcement progress in the sixties. Automated equipment and processes, especially in records-keeping tasks, are essential if the police are to keep pace with and benefit from industrial and commercial technological advances. Finally, some regionalization of police services is essential. Especially is this so in metropolitan areas where population concentration, the mobility of criminal elements and other conditions create special and difficult problems for the police.

Police work has by no means exhausted the law enforcement applications that can be made of man's knowledge in physical science or the social and behavioral sciences. This awesome task can only gather momentum as men conversant with this knowledge and its application are drawn to the police service as a meaningful and rewarding endeavor worthy of their dedication and best efforts. These men, upon whom law enforcement must look to chart the course through the rest of the twentieth century, must be those who have acquired the benefit of college or university and advanced education.

Raised educational standards will not by themselves attract a stream of highly qualified applicants to a police agency. Each department must tell and retell its story if it is to get a response from college prepared men and women. The police must become more actively involved in recruiting. The emphasis should not be on processing applications but on assuring that ample applications are received to process. The people needed are not a special breed who would naturally gravitate toward police work regardless of salaries, standards or recruiting campaigns. There is one pool of individuals who possess the qualifications we seek. Acquiring them is a matter of competing with every agency and industry that seeks their talents. To deny this reality perpetuates the status quo and retards the professionalization of police work. Obviously an agency will not get these people unless it goes after them on the campus and elsewhere dramatizes the police service, the work and its importance and the personal rewards involved.

This is the challenge that confronts law enforcement and this challenge will be particularly felt by municipal, county and state police agencies that have historically commanded more modest salaries and marshalled fewer resources than have federal law enforcement agencies. The present day police situation and the pale reality of increasing crime and public safety problems will hopefully find a growing number of police agencies bringing their plight to the forefront of public attention and championing higher standards in every form. Momentum is a curious thing. Once gained it is able to overcome obstacles and becomes difficult to stop or thwart. So it is with the crying needs of the police service—the necessary momentum is building department by department.

The Multnomah County Sheriff's Police Department has moved ahead on the accomplishments of other law enforcement agencies. As the present process continues and others follow the new lead, we shall be pleased that we had the opportunity to move law enforcement ahead another step. To pioneer is an honor, but the real feeling of accomplishment comes when others follow to move the frontiers further ahead.